inside
basketball

inside basketball

dick barnett

with
augie borgi

Contemporary Books, Inc.
Chicago

Copyright © 1971 by Dick Barnett
Published by Contemporary Books, Inc.
180 North Michigan Avenue, Chicago, Illinois 60601
Manufactured in the United States of America
Library of Congress Catalog Card Number: 77-80518
International Standard Book Number: 0-8092-8861-3 (cloth)
0-8092-8860-5 (paper)

Published simultaneously in Canada by
Beaverbooks
953 Dillingham Road
Pickering, Ontario L1W 1Z7
Canada

Dick Barnett is one of the most knowledgeable men in the National Basketball Association and a definite coaching prospect for the future. He understands the game, likes it, and plays it on both offense and defense. He's probably the smartest basketball player in the league.

—Red Holzman, general manager and coach of the New York Knickerbockers, August 1, 1971.

contents

DETERMINATION...and discipline are part of winning. When I'm up against a tough opponent, as I am here, the worst thing that I can do is show my emotions. I try to keep a cool look on my face so that my opponent won't know that I'm frustrated.

Every American child has shot, bounced, or passed a basketball at some time. And every adult American has watched at least one game.

Today, basketball is no longer the game that James Naismith invented one day in 1891 in a Massachusetts YMCA. Since that day in Springfield, it has developed into a sport that is viewed by millions on national television. When the New York Knickerbockers draw more than one million people for their home games at Madison Square Garden in one season, it doesn't take a mathematical genius to realize that basketball is a game enjoyed by all types of sports fans during the winter months. And it is also a game that most kids play in school during physical education classes.

With this in mind, I am going to attempt to explain the game to you, so that you can watch it more intelligently and play it with some degree of skill—using the age-old theory that everyone enjoys doing something he does well. Before delving into the techniques, however, the younger player should understand something about the game and the equipment he needs to play it. Basketball is more than just two teams with five players each running up and down the court trying to put the ball through an iron rim while preventing their opponents from scoring.

THE COURT

A basketball court (see page 2) can be laid out anywhere. It can be indoors on a hardwood floor, or outdoors on concrete or asphalt. But wherever the court is located, it should be of regulation size. You would hardly expect a twelve-year-old basketball player to have as much endurance as Walt Frazier or Willis Reed. Consequently, the length of the court for grade school and high school games is 10 feet shorter (84 feet) than it is for college and pro games (94 feet). However, all courts have the same 50-foot width.

As a safety precaution for the players who inadvertently run out-of-bounds during play, there should always be 3 feet of unobstructed space beyond the end lines and the sidelines.

The center line, which divides the court into two halves, determines your team's frontcourt and backcourt. The area from your basket to the center line is your team's frontcourt; the other half is considered your backcourt.

The keyhole, or key as it is commonly called, is the area of the free-throw lane. As it is seen from the end line, this area is shaped like a giant keyhole, thus its name. The most important thing to remember about the keyhole, other than the fact that

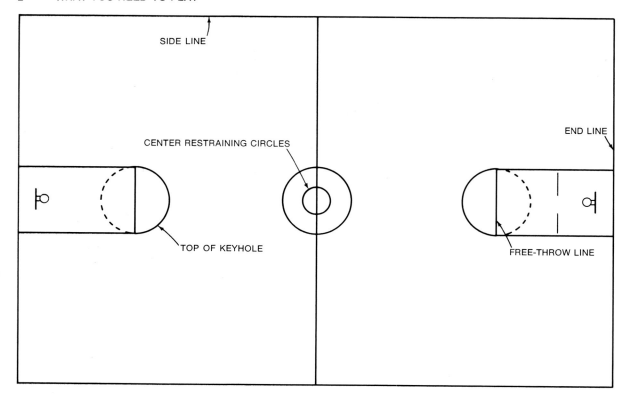

DIAGRAM 1. The Court.

it is the area where you take your free throws (see Chapter 2), is that while your team is in possession of the ball, you cannot remain in this area for more than three seconds.

The circle within a circle at the middle of the court is called the center restraining circle. At this point, the game is started with a jump ball between two players.

THE BASKETBALL

The ball is spherical in shape and should be an approved shade of orange or natural tan color. The best weight is twenty-one ounces, although you might want to pump the ball up to as much as twenty-two ounces, knowing that it will lose air during play.

I don't suggest giving young, beginning players one of the smaller balls that are available for youngsters. If a boy continues to play basketball as he grows up, he will have to change to the larger ball when he enters higher levels of competition. This transition, at such a late date, will be much harder for him. Besides, it is important in ball handling for a young player to learn to spread and stretch his fingers. The best way for him to learn this is to use the larger ball from the beginning.

BASKETS

If you play on a regulation court, the basket (Diagram 2) at either end is constructed of a metal ring, 18 inches in diameter, which supports a net basket. The

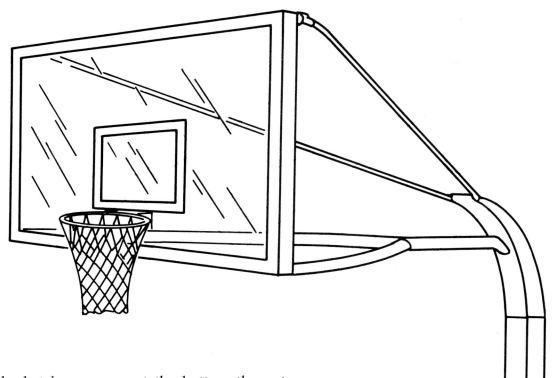

basket is narrower at the bottom than at the top. This narrowing serves to momentarily stop the ball as it passes through the basket. The basket ring, which is 10 feet above the floor, high enough even for tall players, is securely attached to the backboard by a brace. The backboard has to be constructed of a rigid, flat material so that the ball can rebound properly. Heavy metal or plastic is suitable, although backboards constructed for the driveway or backyard are often made of wood.

DIAGRAM 2. The Basket. This type of basket has a rectangular transparent backboard and is one of several kinds used.

OTHER GEAR

Once you have a place to play, such as a school or YMCA gym, a driveway, or backyard, and have two baskets and a ball, all you need are a pair of comfortably fitting gym shoes (either high or low), sweat socks with reinforced soles, and a T-shirt and gym shorts.

If you are playing outside in chilly weather, make sure you are dressed warmly. However, don't wear too much clothing because as you play your body will warm up. It's not good to shed clothes in an attempt to cool off; your body temperature will drop suddenly, and you will become chilled. Just don't wear too much in the beginning.

If you wear a knee support make sure that it fits properly. If it's too loose, it will slide around; but if it's too tight, it will cut off your circulation, which is worse.

Players who wear glasses should use a safety guard. This device is attached to the sides of your glasses and drawn around your head to hold the glasses in position so they can't be knocked off as you play.

KNOW THE RULES

I can't overemphasize how important it is for you not only to *learn* the rules, but to *know* them thoroughly. You can handicap your team as much by not knowing the rules as you can by not knowing how to shoot and score.

With a thorough knowledge of the rules, you can avoid penalties and especially fouls that can eliminate you from the play entirely if you commit five in one game.

Basketball rules vary for different kinds of players, and you should learn the ones that apply to you whether you are a grade school, high school, college, amateur, or professional player. The appendix at the back of the book lists addresses that you can write to for a rule book. If you don't already have a thorough knowledge of the game, write for your book today, and start studying.

IT'S A TEAM GAME

It took the Knicks twenty-four years to win a world's championship. It probably took the same number of years for the New York sports world to realize that the only way to play the game of basketball is to play it as a team game.

Wilt Chamberlain once averaged 50 points a game and, undoubtedly, is the greatest scorer ever to play basketball. Oscar Robertson, it has been said many times, is the greatest individual to play the game, but Oscar, like Wilt, at this writing has never been on a world's championship team. One player does not make a team. One player does not win championships. One player cannot do it alone. Five players and a capable bench, guided by an astute coach, are needed to win a championship, especially on the professional level.

When the Knicks won their championship, they won it with a fine five-man effort from the starting cast, which consisted of Willis Reed, Dave DeBusschere, Bill Bradley, Walt Frazier, and myself. The bench, which sportswriters called the greatest this side of the Supreme Court, consisted of Mike Riordan, Cazzie Russell, Donnie May, Bill Hosket, Dave Stallworth, Johnny Warren, and Nate Bowman. We played together under coach Red Holzman, using the fundamentals of the game as our guide to consistent winning.

Determination and discipline are part of winning.

The good player never shows his emotions outwardly. He never shows emotions until the game is won. He never gives the other team the advantage of knowing that he may be flustered. Because a championship team never seems to show any emotion, it always seems to have complete control.

Members of championship teams are constantly in motion, making the proper plays. This means the good player knows what he is attempting to do at all times. He plays basketball with the other members of his team, as part of the team effort.

IT'S A TEAM GAME. Basketball games aren't won by individuals;
they must be a team effort. Here Willis Reed (19) goes up for a jump ball supported
by Cazzie Russell (33) and Walt Frazier (behind 18).

IN THE CLUTCH.
Sportswriters call me a "clutch" shooter because I'm always able to make shots when we need points. But shooting accuracy depends on getting the right spot on the floor and then going up for the shot in an easy, controlled manner.

chapter 2
SHOOTING

The only way to score points in basket-ball is by shooting, and the basic purpose in offense is to free a man for an open shot. When any player receives the ball, he must be *able* to shoot. Just as basketball is a five-man effort in terms of rebounding, guarding, and passing, it is also a five-player effort in terms of shooting. The player who cannot shoot is a luxury few teams can afford.

True, some players are better shooters than others and some receive recognition for their defense and rebounding. Bill Russell, who turned the Boston Celtics into a perennial championship team during the height of his career, was not noted for his scoring. Yet, he still scored 15,000 points during his National Basketball Association days.

Putting the ball into the iron rim that extends from the 10-foot-high backboard is the primary object of basketball. The team that does it most, wins. So the player who can't score consistently will be a weak spot in his team and an asset to the opposi-tion. If you can't shoot, you can't play this game.

The closer a player is to the basket, the greater are his chances of scoring. And, of course, when the player with the ball has given his guard the slip, scoring becomes that much easier.

THE LAY-UP

The easiest shot is the lay-up. Since it is an easy shot, keep it that way. Don't at-tempt to make it difficult by using any spin on the shot. The lay-up is the first shot an elementary player should learn. If a player can't make this one, it is likely he can't make any others. Perfect the lay-up before trying to develop other shots.

If you are shooting with your right hand, go up off your left foot and use your right foot for "climbing." Use your left hand as a balancing hand while your right hand guides the ball up to the board. The left-handed shooter uses his right hand as his guide hand and his left hand as his shoot-ing hand. His right foot will be his takeoff foot, and his left foot will be his "climbing" foot. One of the most important things to remember in shooting, or whenever you handle the ball, is fingertip control. In shooting, the fingers act as a fine "guiding system" to get the ball directly to the target —the basket. You cannot develop a "soft touch" in shooting when your palms are on the ball. Just as in any other shot, get the ball up to a comfortable eye level so that you can see the 2-point shot you are mak-ing. Shoot overhand whenever possible.

You take a lay-up under two conditions. First, when you are all alone under the basket and want to take the simplest shot possible. Since it is easier to use the backboard as a convenient, soft bank-shot, you should move off to one side or the other as you make the shot. If you are a right-handed player, move to the right side of the basket and place the ball on the board so that your body is positioned between your shooting arm and your defender. This positioning protects the ball and allows it to drop gently into the hoop. If you are left-handed, move to the left side and follow the same procedure.

The percentages of making the shot improve if you shoot from the right side with your right hand and the left side with your left hand. But the good player learns to shoot with *both* hands, so that he will be able to make the best percentage shot at all times.

Second, use the underhand lay-up when you want to force the man defending you to commit a foul by "hacking" your shooting arm. In this case, you are going to drive—that is, dribble the ball in such a manner as to advance around the defense —for a lay-up. You can also use the lay-up when you have a half-step advantage over the defender.

When shooting from in front of the basket with the defensive man closing in, use a two-hand underhand lay-up shot. It is more difficult to score with this shot than when you shoot from the left or right side. However, one advantage is that your body protects the ball from the defensive player.

A relaxed shooter seldom misses a lay-up. This is especially true when a pass is intercepted. The resulting unmolested shot —the lay-up—after a long dribble is almost always 2 points. In fact, lay-ups, statisticians tell me, are made 86 percent of the time by high school players and 92 percent of the time by professional players. Missed lay-ups occur when a player is too tense and slams the ball off the backboard.

Follow the proper takeoff position with your hands and feet, and guide the ball up for a soft, almost impossible to miss shot. Try to shoot the ball overhand; it will re-

LAY-UP FORM. When I go up for a lay-up with my right hand, I go up off my left foot and climb with my right leg. In the follow-through, my arm will be fully extended.

good, adds 1 more point to the score, giving the offense 3 points for that play.)

Without bragging, I might mention that I probably make more 3-point plays at crucial times than anyone else in pro ball, and I specialize in delaying my shot so that the man guarding me will foul me just as I am shooting.

Naturally, you should not wait for the defender to block your shot. Nor should you delay long enough to miss your lay-up. Only when you have mastered both the lay-up and the delaying technique should you attempt to create a 3-point play. The free throw is only a bonus. Actually, it is a double bonus: fouls put the defensive player in foul trouble. A defensive player must leave the game when he commits five fouls. By hesitating and forcing him to foul, you are actually quickening his exit from the game under the personal foul quota.

Finally, of course, you must be a proficient foul shooter. The poor free-throw shooter should not even think of using this delaying shot.

TAP-IN

Do not confuse the lay-up with the tap-in, which is used after a shot is missed. With a tap-in, one of the offensive players (usually the center because he is most often the tallest) jumps up to tap the rebounding ball of a missed shot through the net. The tap-in is not considered a shot because it does not originate with the player who makes it. The player making the tap-in actually is working off one of his teammates' shots.

DUNK SHOT

When I am alone under the basket, the lay-up is the shot I take before any other.

DESPITE OPPOSITION...Walt Frazier goes up for his lay-up. This is a perfect example of a 3-point opportunity.

duce misses whenever the defensive player is near.

When you make an underhand lay-up, the defender stands a good chance of fouling you, which can result in a 3-point play. (A 3-point play occurs when a player makes a basket for 2 points and at the same time is fouled by a defender. This foul entitles him to a free throw, which, if

Some players use a dunk, or stuff shot—meaning jumping from the floor and jamming the ball into the hoop from above the rim. This requires good jumping ability and wastes considerable energy. (In high school and college basketball, the dunk shot is illegal, and there is a technical foul for using it.)

I can dunk the ball, but I feel the lay-up is just as effective. It may not thrill the crowd, but it does count for the same 2 points as the dunk shot. Some of the big players of the game — people like Wilt Chamberlain, Lew Alcindor, Willis Reed — draw great applause by dunking the ball. But New York fans still remember how many times Walt Bellamy missed dunk shots and how Cazzie Russell missed dunk shots during playoff games against the Milwaukee Bucks. The dunk shot is flamboyant, but flamboyance is not worth a miss. The lay-up is rarely a missed shot.

POSITION FOR CONTROL. Have your shooting hand under the ball (the left here) and use the other hand as a guide. By positioning your shooting hand so that you form a V with your thumb and index finger, you have greater control of the ball.

SHOOTING WITH ONE HAND

When you are too far from the basket to take a lay-up, the one-hand shot gives you both speed and accuracy. The guide hand and the shooting hand are used in the same fashion as in the lay-up. One hand will guide the ball, the other will do the actual pushing or shooting.

The *one-hand jump shot* must be part of your repertoire if you are going to be a good scorer. This shot is similar to the lay-up in that one hand does the shooting and the other is used for balance.

Whether you jump straight up in the air, toward the basket, or away from it depends on how closely you are being guarded. The most difficult time to shoot is when you are going backward, that is, away from the basket.

Let us assume you are jumping straight up in the air. You can take off with both feet or with just the left foot. If you take off with both feet, both legs will be extended as you jump off the floor. If you take off with your left foot, your left leg will be extended while the right leg is bent. This bent leg may protect you against your defender. It will discourage him from playing you too tightly. However, you can be charged with an offensive foul if you use your leg like a battering ram.

Remember to release the ball at the top of your jump. This should be a high-type jump, not a long one. Go up in the air as high as you can, and shoot the ball at the top of your jump, getting the ball above eye level before letting go of it, so you can see the basket clearly and so the defender will have to go that much higher in an effort to block your shot. Do not shoot the ball on your way down.

If you can fake your defender into thinking you are going to shoot, he will come off his feet in an attempt to block your shot.

Then when he is on his downward flight to the floor, you should go up for your shot.

How do you fake your man?

1. Twist your head upward so that he will think you are going into the air.

2. Throw your hands up with the ball, but keep your feet on the floor.

FALL BACK, BABY! This is my famous one-hand jump shot, which I have been using throughout my professional career. I jump in the air, with my hands above my head directing the ball toward the basket. Then, leaning back, I take my shot as I start to come down.

JUMP SHOT

Many years ago in the schoolyard games in Gary, Indiana, I developed my own, somewhat unique, one-hand jump shot. I curl my legs behind my body and shoot the ball as I am coming down. However, this is a rather unorthodox way to shoot and is not recommended.

The correct way to shoot a jump shot is at the height of your jump. I do not possess great jumping ability, so I perfected my shot by letting it go a split second after the defender expects it to be taken. Hence, I am shooting the ball on my downward flight. Sportswriters dubbed this my "fall back, baby" shot because I actually yelled "Fall back, baby!" during my younger playing days. This was a signal to my teammates that I was making a basket, and they should be prepared to play defense. In this unique, off-balance shot, I was actually falling backward. Many times, I would end up flat on my back, sprawled out on the floor. But falling on the floor didn't hurt my chances for drawing a free throw, either!

Young players can use the jump shot as a method of drawing fouls. Until the NBA referees began calling offensive fouls on me, I would fake my man out of position for a jump shot and then jump into him as I went up for my shot. The result: a 3-point opportunity. That opportunity still exists for the high school player and 99 percent of the college players, because their referees are inclined to call the foul against the defender, who was feinted, or faked, out of position.

If the defensive player does not respond to a fake, the jump shot should be delayed because the offensive player cannot afford to take a shot that he knows he can't make. He should dribble or fake again. He must never stand still.

The Pros Create Shots

Oscar Robertson and Jerry West are the greatest jump shooters of the game. They serve as perfect models for the young player. Copy them.

When West receives the ball, he takes that first quick step so that the defender is immediately backpedaling, or rushing back, to get into a good defensive position. And while the defender is occupied with going backward, West is at the height of his jump, releasing his jump shot, one of the best in the game.

A national television audience and a capacity crowd at The Forum in Los Angeles saw Jerry West's uncanny shooting during the 1970 playoffs. With three seconds to play and the score tied, David De Busschere of the Knicks made a shot to give New York a 2-point lead. Immediately, Wilt Chamberlain passed the ball in bounds and headed for the dressing room before the sellout crowd could surround him and block his path. Then, while the fans were thinking about getting to their cars for the trip home on the freeway, West did the impossible. He sank a 65-foot jump shot to send the game into overtime.

Jerry went up off his left foot, using his right foot to climb into the air. He set the ball on his right hand, using the left as a guide to balance it. He raised the ball up to eye level and released the shot, following through with his right hand. Just before he made this spectacular shot, I was making it difficult for him to dribble. But Willis Reed was making it hard for West to go to his left, so he was forced to the right, where I was ready for his shot.

Yes, West made the shot. Classic. It was not a desperation throw. The ball was shot according to the fundamentals of shooting.

I have told sportswriters that there is only one way to guard Jerry West: "Keep your body between him and the ball; keep your hand in his eyes; don't allow him to be more than a half step away from you; and don't allow him to get the ball. Then you have to hope he misses." I am not exaggerating. This is the way you have to defense pro players well drilled in fundamentals.

Oscar Robertson is even more difficult than Jerry West to guard because he is physically so much stronger. This is not to say West is not strong. He has strength, but in a wiry sense. West has been hampered by many injuries, ranging from broken noses to pulled hamstring muscles, which may have resulted from his quick shots that often catch defenders rushing back a split second before he releases the ball. As they recover and come back into him, his shot already arching to the hoop, he gets fouled —often getting a 3-point play but also getting injured.

Oscar, too, gets the 3-point plays, but in a different way. His is, more or less, the same technique I use to make some of my jump shots: we both try to draw a violation that will give us a free throw and our defenders personal fouls.

Robertson attempts to make the defender move first. The idea is to fake with the ball. If the defensive man responds to the fake, the offensive player has an advantage. If the defender doesn't, the offensive player still hasn't lost anything.

If the defensive player goes for the fake and leaves his feet, the offensive player has a perfect opportunity to go up for his jump shot. While the defender is coming down and in no position to block the shot, the shooter is going up, leaving the floor with both feet so that he can reach a maximum height. His shoulders are square, and the ball is guided with both hands and then released from the shooting hand.

THE TWO-HAND SHOT

The two-hand shot isn't as popular today as it once was, primarily because of the great accuracy and speed of the one-hand shot. However, it does have a place in the game and is an excellent shot to attempt from long distances. It is also good for the young player who is having difficulty perfecting a one-hand foul shot.

In taking a shot with both hands, keep both feet on the floor and get the ball up to eye level so the defender will have to be extremely fast to block the shot, which will be traveling high all the time. With the

TWO-HAND SHOT. In attempting a two-hand set shot, I balance the ball above my head with both hands. This shot is especially good for long distances, and the higher you keep your hands above your head, the more difficult it is for the defender to block your shot.

two-hand shot, the elbows are extended away from the body and the hands are up high. An upside-down V is formed, with the ball at the point where the arms and hands come together to form the V. As in other shots, the ball is released with finger-tip control. The arms are used in this shot for power. This shot can be attempted from distances of 35 to 40 feet by a player who has developed strong wrists.

The two-hand shot requires more time for proper execution than a one-hand shot. Consequently, it is a shot that won't be attempted too often during a game, except at the foul line.

Red Holzman, the Knicks' coach, amazed some of the younger players one day by sinking a two-hand set shot 45 feet from the basket. Everyone asked what kind of shot it was. "It was a two-hand shot," I told a reporter at the practice session. "I saw one in the movies once when I was a boy."

The two-hand shot is not a required one to know. But it can win or lose a game, so practice it.

THE HOOK SHOT

For every fifty one-hand or jump shots a player attempts, he may take one hook shot.

George Mikan made the hook shot famous when the Lakers were a championship team in Minneapolis. Today, its use has gradually disappeared from the game. Still, it is a valuable shot and should be learned by every player.

I enjoy using the hook shot because it draws fouls and is therefore doubly useful. Moreover, because the defender is looking for a one-hand or jump shot and is positioning himself to block the shot he expects, the hook can be extremely successful since the defender is off guard.

A PERFECT HOOK. Willis Reed (19) applies everything he knows about the fundamentals of shooting when he makes his hook. Notice how he keeps his body between his shooting arm and his defender, making it impossible for the Chicago Bulls' player to block his shot.

The hook shot is taken with the hand farthest from the basket and the shooter's back to the hoop. The shooter's body is usually between the ball and the defender. The arm with the ball is extended away from the body and brought up to shooting level—the best possible location above eye level—and released gently.

Unless the defensive player is a great deal taller than the shooter, it is almost impossible to block the hook. Height advantages and the proficiency of the shooter make the hook a good percentage shot. When the shooter has a height advantage, he can move in closer to the basket while the defender prepares himself for the expected jump shot.

In most instances the ball should be banked off the backboard, just as in a layup. It is advisable to learn the hook shot using either hand, remembering that the left hand will be used as both a ball guide for the right-handed shooter and as protection from the defensive player who is playing tightly. When the left-handed hook is attempted, the right hand becomes the guide and is kept between the defender and the ball. Being able to shoot a hook with either hand aids the shooter in that it makes his fakes or feints more effective.

Shoot the hook with a full sweeping motion of the arm, which should be almost straight. Your eyes should be on the target, just as in every shot taken in basketball.

The arc of the hook shot varies with the individual. Never is the ball to be banged off the backboard. The ball should not be shot in line-drive fashion. It should be gently arched to the basket.

The hook shot requires more practice than any other shot with the exception of the free throw—one of the most important shots in the game since it is taken without interference from defensive action.

FOUL SHOOTING

Only when you are on the foul line—15 feet from the basket, handed the ball by the referee, and given ten seconds to attempt a free throw—are you permitted an absolutely open shot. And, strangely enough, pro teams make only 70 percent of their foul shots, the better players converting 80 percent of their free throws into points.

This is where most games, especially on the amateur level, are won and lost. The following tips will help you to improve your free throw accuracy.

1. Don't think about any other phase of of the game, such as the score, when you are foul shooting.

2. Your body should be perfectly balanced. Weight should be distributed on the balls of your feet.

3. Relax at the foul line by bouncing the ball on the floor so that you gain a a comfortable "feel" for the shot.

4. Aim for the front of the rim and take a deep breath. Try to shoot so that the ball will just glide over the rim. If your shot is short, it may hit the front of the rim and drop into the cords.

5. Shoot the ball softly. Do not fire the ball so rapidly that it will hit the rim and rebound wildly.

6. Use the foul shot technique that is consistently successful for you. Various techniques on how to make foul shots are explained in this chapter. You can take your choice. You should have an assortment of techniques, but stick to a few good ones rather than a lot that are mediocre.

DIAGRAM 3. In a foul shooting situation two of your teammates must alternate positions with four players from the other team. Occupying the wrong space adjacent to the end line is a violation.

Developing Technique

An old axiom, "practice makes perfect," can be applied appropriately to foul shooting.

In the free throw, the hands are placed directly behind the ball. The fingers are spread in such a way as to form a strong arc across the sides of the ball from the tip of the little finger, across the back of the hand, and out through the thumb.

The knees are bent. The ball is bounced once or twice for relaxation and control and then brought to eye level. Beginning with a slight push from the knees, feet remaining on the floor as much as possible, the wrists unlock and the ball is released from the fingertips. The arms and fingers guide the ball toward the basket, and the elbows remain away from the body and straighten out in the follow through.

This procedure is not really complicated once you begin to practice your foul shooting. It is a simple method of shooting, especially when no one is guarding you. Unfortunately, a 15-foot shot is not really easy for the average person and takes considerable practice.

After taking two foul shots, step away from the line. You will never take more than two foul shots at a time in a game on the amateur level and never more than three on the professional level.

Some basketball players can make twenty-five shots in a row when they are concluding their daily practice sessions. They can also make nearly all of their shots in a pregame warm-up *once* they have found their range. Yet, they have difficulty with foul shooting during a game.

Why?

Like a bowler who finds a groove during

ON THE LINE. Before I take my free throw,
I hold the ball in both hands and bounce it
a few times to get the feel of it.
Then, bending my knee slightly, I concentrate
on the shot I am about to take.

100% CONCENTRATION. After I have bounced
the ball on the floor a few times for control,
I bring it up to eye level and bend one knee, keeping
my right foot back and my elbows out. Then I push
off with my left foot and arc the ball toward the hoop.

practice but has trouble finding the pocket during actual competition when he must wait for other members of the team to roll their shots, the foul shooter finds a groove during practice, but finds it much more difficult to shoot the same way under game conditions.

During a game, a player is offered two free throws. He doesn't have time to find the proper groove. For this reason, do your free throw practicing under game conditions. Find the rhythm of your shooting. After taking your two shots, step back away from the line. Then return. Bounce the ball to get the feel of it. Relax. Take a deep breath. Concentrate on the rim, and take your "soft" shot.

Foul shooting is mechanical. It is merely practice. A foul shot is an open, free shot. No one can stop you.

In my free throw I use a one-hand shot and aim for an imaginary spot just over the front of the rim. Since no one is going to try to block my shot, I get into a comfortable position, putting one foot behind the other while gently resting the ball in my shooting hand (my left). I use my other hand as a guide to balance the ball as I raise it to shoot.

I bend my knees and focus my eyes on the front of the rim. My shoulders are squared so that I have complete balance in my shot. My arms guide the ball up to eye level, and I raise the ball over my head. My shooting hand lofts the ball toward the basket as my wrist unlocks to provide the power to get the ball into flight.

POSITION SHOOTING

The floor position from where you shoot and the type of shot you take depend on factors such as: Which offensive system is your team using? What is your best shot?

How close is the defensive player guarding you? What is the score of the game? How much time remains in the game? How close are you to the basket, and can you make a good shot? How good a shooter are you?

But regardless of any of these factors in a given situation, a good player must be able to shoot from any place on the floor—regardless of what position he plays.

Some coaches want certain players to shoot from certain positions on the floor, that is, the forwards shoot from the corners, the center from underneath the basket and in the lane, and the guards from the backcourt or on drives to the basket. Moreover, the players are positioned by the coach for good reason. It makes sense for the bigman—or the center as he is called by oldtimers and the public address men who announce lineups to the crowd—to do more shooting than the other players if he has a height advantage or is a particularly good shooter.

Today, however, the formal designation of position means very little. The guards must be able to shoot from the corners, and the forwards must be able to shoot from the backcourt area. The terms center, forward, and guard are gradually losing their meaning in the basketball world of today.

Willis Reed of the Knicks is an excellent example of this. He can shoot from under the basket, or he can move out into one of the corners and still shoot accurately 30 feet away from the hoop. He can also go into the foul circle and shoot well from the middle of the floor.

But Willis is no different from any other pro player. Bill Bradley made shots from the area under the basket during his college days. Now he is shooting from long range because, at 6'5", he is one of the shorter professional players.

The young player should learn to shoot from any spot on the floor. Don't designate yourself as a cornerman or a bigman or a backcourtman. You may be tall for the games at your school but short for games at another school. When Walt Frazier was a sophomore in high school, he was the center. When he was a junior, he became a guard.

PRACTICE ROUTINE

The next time you go to a game or watch one on television, watch the pros as they warm up. They don't come out on the floor and jog around without a purpose. They practice the shots they expect to take in the game. The young player should do likewise.

During warmup the bigmen shoot from underneath the basket and gradually work their way outside. The cornermen practice shots from the 18-foot areas on the side and corners and drive to the hoop. Eventually they take some jump shots. The guards shoot from the top of the foul circle area and then go into the corners for some 20-foot shots. Then, they work on driving to the hoop for some lay-ups. All players practice foul shooting no matter what size they are or what position they play.

YEARS, HOURS, MINUTES

The pros have been practicing their shooting for years. The young player may spend twenty minutes on a shot when he begins playing. Eventually he'll spend hours developing it.

Bill Bradley would take two hundred shots from the same spot on the floor when he was a young boy. Other pro players did the same thing as youngsters. The good shooter practices long, hard, and intelligently. If a player can't shoot, he can't play this game.

TIPS ON SHOOTING

- Concentrate on your target.
- Look at the rim as you shoot, and follow through.
- Be perfectly balanced. Keep your weight on the balls of your feet.
- Hold the ball so that you will have fingertip control.
- Keep the palms of your hands off the ball.
- Develop strong wrists.
- Practice your shot so that your aim becomes instinctive.
- Anticipate. Always know what you want to do.

FAKE YOUR MAN. Whenever you are being heavily defended going toward the hoop, pass off to an outside teammate in a better position to make the shot. Here, my defender has already jumped up to block my shot, but I fake him by passing to Walt Frazier (10), who has a much better shooting position.

chapter 3
PASSING

In basketball the scorer receives most of the publicity and the attention, but before a score can be made there must be a pass. In most cases, there will be more than one pass before any points are made.

A team that can pass is a team that can win championships. The Knicks proved just how important passing is to winning when they won their first championship in twenty-four years with a deft display of passing that knowledgeable basketball people termed: "beautiful."

True, the scorer gets the recognition in the newspapers, but the passer gets the satisfaction of knowing he set up the goal or play that resulted in a basket or some opportunity at the foul line.

If you can't pass, you run the risk of costing your team 4 points for every bad or incomplete pass you make. Think of it this way: if you lose possession of the ball, your team loses the chance to score 2 points, and the other team gets that opportunity. This is a 4-point differential. For this reason, basketball statisticians believe possession of the ball is worth 1½ points.

The prime purpose of the game is to outscore the opposition; this can't be done unless a team establishes a passing pattern that will provide the opportunity to shoot and score points.

Each pass should be made with a flick of the wrists and a push from the fingers and thumbs. The arms and elbows should be straightened in the follow through. There should be a slight backward spin on the ball, just as in shooting. However, too little spin on the ball results when your wrists are locked, too much spin results when you snap your wrists but allow your fingers to be too relaxed.

TWO-HAND PASSES

Passing can be broken down into two categories: two-hand passes and one-hand passes. You should follow through on passes, just as you do on shots. Remember that a pass travels four times faster than a dribble, so when you have a choice between the two, it is usually better to pass.

Two-hand passes are used mostly when

SNAP THE PASS. As you pass the ball, flick
your wrists and extend your fingers and arms.
Follow through, directing the ball
to your receiver.

you want an accurate pass over a short distance. The receiver must be within a 15- to 20-foot range. Two-hand passes include the chest pass, bounce pass, the lob, and the shovel pass.

Chest Pass

In throwing a simple two-hand chest pass, the ball is held in a position at chest level. The fingers are comfortably spread on both sides of the ball, but more toward the back, with your palms off the ball. (Remember, all ball handling is done with the fingertips.) The elbows remain close to the body at approximately waist level.

As you step toward your intended receiver, extend your arms and release the ball with a snap of the wrists and a push of the thumbs. This release propels the ball toward the receiver in the same spinning fashion as in shooting. Use your thumbs to put a backward rotation on the ball. The step forward, taken at the beginning of the pass, helps in the follow through and gives you more accuracy.

This type of pass—the chest pass—is used for short distances of approximately 15 feet or less when you need to be accurate. For long distance shots, getting the ball from one end of the court to the other, use a one-hand pass.

Bounce Pass

Once you have mastered the chest pass, you are ready for the bounce pass, an ideal two-hand pass used against zone defenses, which will be discussed in detail in Chapter 7.

The bounce pass should be delivered in the same manner as the two-hand chest pass. However, instead of throwing the ball directly to the receiver, you bounce it at a point on the floor about two-thirds of the way between you and the receiver. This bounce enables the receiver to catch the ball in a low position approximately at knee level. If the bounce pass is aimed at a higher level than the knee, it is easy for a defensive player to intercept the ball.

As you release the ball with a push of your thumbs, put a backward spin, or rotation, on it by flicking your wrists down and back. This backward rotation makes the ball bounce true. A forward rotation, or spin, makes the ball takeoff in odd directions and confuses the receiver.

Before making a bounce pass, sight your receiver. Sight the spot on the floor where you will throw the ball so that it will

BOUNCE PASS. If I bounce the ball about two-thirds of the way toward my receiver, he is able to catch it in a low position. A low ball is less likely to get out of control than a high one. This is especially important when you are being rushed by defenders.

bounce directly to him. A warning: Do not overuse the bounce pass. The defensive players will begin to anticipate it and will start making interceptions.

Lob Pass

The lob pass, like the bounce pass, is used to get around or past the defense. The word "lob" means to propel in a high arc. This is precisely the motion of the ball in this pass.

The position of the feet and hands in the lob pass is the same as in the two-hand chest and bounce passes. The primary difference is that the ball is held directly over the head with both arms extended and the elbows slightly bent. The momentum is supplied by a snap of the wrists, a downward extension of the arms (stopping at shoulder level), and the push from the fingers and thumbs. At the same time, the passer should step forward and put the strength of his shoulders behind the ball. Aim just over the receiver's head or at his chin if there is no defensive man around.

The lob pass usually is used by the taller players on the team. A successful lob pass over the head of the fronting defender will give the receiver a clear path to the basket for a possible lay-up.

This pass can be used successfully when applying a fake. If you are standing some distance from the basket and want to get the ball in closer, you can fake a shot and lob pass the ball over the head of your defender to your receiver, who can then make the shot. Just as the bounce pass is useful in getting the ball to the bigman under the basket, the lob pass is ideal for getting the ball inside when the defending pivotman is fronting (playing in front of his man, rather than between his man and the basket).

In faking, get the ball up above eye level as if you are going to shoot. This lures your

LOB PASS. On a throw-in from out-of-bounds, I use a lob pass to get over my defender, who is ready to jump up to get the ball. Notice that I am holding the ball correctly: over my head with my elbows slightly bent.

defender and the defender of the intended receiver. As they look for the shot, release the ball with a slow arc so that at first it appears to be a shot. Use your wrists to lift the ball so that your defender can't block the pass, but make the pass gentle enough so that it will descend in the intended receiver's hands and out of the fronting defender's reach.

Obviously, the lob pass requires perfect timing. It can't be overused. But the chances of interception with this pass are much greater than with the chest or bounce pass, so protect the ball.

Shovel Pass

The shovel pass is used to get the ball to a player who is cutting toward the basket. When using the shovel pass, keep your hands firmly on the ball, and keep your feet wide apart. Bend your body forward.

As you hold the ball, your teammate comes by within a 3- to 5-foot range, and

you scoop or "shovel" the ball to him. The ball is shoveled in a sweeping motion. This is probably the shortest pass you will throw, but it is one that gives the player cutting to the basket an easy shot.

ONE-HAND PASSES

One-hand passes are used to cover greater distances. They are not as accurate as two-hand passes, but they do get the ball down the court.

Before you attempt to throw these long distance passes, which the professional players use, remember that the pros have much larger hands and are probably much stronger than you are. Have some mastery of two-hand passes before practicing the one-hand passes. Remember, if you can pass with either hand, you will have an advantage over the player who can pass with only one hand.

In this section, one-hand passes will be described in terms of the right-handed player. The left-handed passer simply must reverse the instructions.

Baseball Pass

The one-hand pass puts speed into the ball. This is important when a team is taking the ball out-of-bounds and wants to make a quick pass before the defense adjusts. The technique most commonly used is termed the baseball pass because the ball is thrown like a baseball. The passer steps forward with his left foot and brings his right hand back behind his right shoulder. He is careful not to step inbounds until after the ball is released. The baseball pass can be thrown long distances with a good degree of accuracy.

In throwing the baseball pass, plant your back foot in a good position for balance. Use this foot to put power in your pass by pushing your weight forward as you release the ball. Throw the ball overhand from behind your shoulder. This gives it speed and helps the ball travel in a straight line. Snap your wrist forward and down. Don't allow your wrist to break either to the right or left. If it does, the pass will not be straight. A sidearm pass—throwing the ball from your hip or side instead of from behind your shoulder—will cause the ball to curve.

Bowling or Underhand Pass

When you want to pass a fast ball on a low level, use the bowling, or underhand pass. Step forward with your left foot, the left shoulder and arm following. Spread your fingers comfortably at the base of the ball.

BASEBALL PASS. In throwing the one-hand baseball pass, bring your passing arm back and extend your other arm out in front of you for leverage and balance. Then, as you bring the ball forward, release it and follow through in the direction of your receiver.

Swing the right arm, extended down at full length, back slightly for momentum. Your left side in its forward position protects the ball from the defender. The receiver catches the ball just below waist level. In this pass, do not snap the wrist either to the left or right. You want a straight pass.

Hook Pass

The hook pass is thrown like the hook shot. The right-handed passer holds the ball slightly behind his right hip. The right hand controls the ball, and the left hand guides it and keeps the defensive player away from the ball. This does not mean that the left hand is used to push the defender. On the contrary, it is used as a protective device to impede the defender. That is, the defender must foul you to reach the ball.

The passer takes one step with his left foot (away from the defensive man), brings the ball up, passes directly overhead with his right hand, and snaps his wrist as he pushes downward.

Behind-the-Back Pass

Like the hook pass, the behind-the-back pass should only be attempted by the experienced player who can control the ball and his body. Naturally, both of these passes require a great deal of practice.

The behind-the-back pass is used for a purpose. It isn't used to be fancy or to impress the crowd. This pass is used in close quarters to pass around a defensive player.

In executing the behind-the-back pass get the ball out so that the defender thinks he has a chance of intercepting it. Make sure your body is in a position to protect the ball. As the defender approaches, your fingertips should be firmly on the ball, and all your weight should be shifted to your passing-arm side. Swing your hips from the

BEHIND-THE-BACK PASS. Walt Frazier, looking at the ball and ready to receive my pass, is just close enough for the behind-the-back pass.
I used this here as a deceptive maneuver against the opponents who were waiting for us upcourt.

right to the left (similar to a golfer's swing), and sweep the ball behind your body. At the last moment, release the ball with fingertip control to the intended open-man receiver. If he is not open, don't throw a behind-the-back pass because it can be intercepted easily.

Overhand Flip and Underarm Passes

The overhand flip pass and the underarm pass are related, not because they are thrown in the same manner, but because it is often possible to fake one and then use the other. Both of these passes are useful for the center or bigman on a team.

In the flip pass, you have assumed your floor position with your back to the basket, feet apart, buttocks out, and the ball out in front of you. Your defender is behind you and is ready to take possession of the ball at any time, so hold it securely in both hands before you make the pass.

One hand is on top of the ball, and one hand is under it. Which hand you use to pass the ball depends on the direction you want to pass. If you want to pass to the left, use the right-hand flip pass. Extend the right arm across your body, and pass the ball to your teammates by snapping your wrist and flipping your fingers. If passing to the right, make the pass in the same way using your left hand.

In the left-hand underarm pass, drop the left arm out, as if you are going to pass to the left, then quickly bring it to the right, snap the wrist, and release the ball under the right arm to your cutter. Learn to fake or pass in either direction so your opponents will not be able to anticipate the direction of your pass.

Handoff

When your receiver cuts close enough to you, you can give him the ball in a simple handoff. This maneuver is similar to a football play where the quarterback hands the ball to a halfback who is passing him closely in the backfield. The handoff adds deception to your attack. You can fake a handoff and then pass to another teammate, or you can fake a handoff and drive around your defender for a lay-up.

The handoff is not to be shrugged off as too simple. It must be completed quickly and deftly. Because it confuses the defense, the handoff can be used to buy a little time as your team moves in toward the basket.

Jump Pass

The jump pass is similar to the jump shot. This pass can be used to get the ball inside to the taller players and to lure the defending players out to the ball.

Cup the ball in your shooting hand, and get your fingers under it. Feint, or fake, to the left and right so your defender, expecting you to shoot, will fall back to protect the basket. Then, holding the ball firmly, leap as high as you can, keeping your shoulders square, and raising the ball up to eye level. Without hesitation, snap your wrist and push your fingers so the ball will move quickly to the receiver.

The defender will not know you are going to pass until the last second. By then it is too late.

Backflip Pass

The same body motion used in the jump pass is used in the backflip pass. However, instead of throwing the ball forward, you toss it to a receiver behind you.

Obviously, this pass is used only when your receiver is away from his defender. Your teammate catches the pass and uses your body as a screen. If he is within shooting range, he probably has a perfect opportunity. When your receiver-shooter is open, you don't have to jump in the air to get your pass over the defender. You simply flip it over your shoulder.

JUMP PASS. Here I've lured Jimmy Walker (24) and Steve Mix of the Pistons by faking a drive.
This leaves Willis Reed, right, open for an easy jump shot when I pass the ball to him.

PASSING DRILLS

The most widely known passing drill is the fast break. The fast break occurs when the defensive team suddenly gains possession of the ball and immediately, in a fast and rapid fashion, races to the basket before the other team can recover and begin to defend properly. Three players rushing offensively on a fast break with only two defenders guarding against a score is an obvious advantage for the offensive team.

Take time out from shooting to practice the fast break. Only three players are necessary to learn this. One player should position himself in the middle of the floor, and the other two should be to the right and left of the middleman. Racing up and down the court, the three players should make quick, accurate passes so that the ball is advanced toward the basket and never touches the floor.

The good fast break team does not dribble the ball; it passes the ball and advances it forward. The ball is always returned to the middleman in the center of the floor. This tactic keeps the ball moving across the entire court and prevents the defensive players from trapping the ball on one side.

In practicing the fast break, move as rapidly as possible. Make sharp, concise passes and try for a lay-up. After making the basket, grab the ball, step out-of-bounds, and fire it inbounds so that your team can make another fast break down the court toward the other basket. Streak toward the basket; don't allow the ball to touch the floor.

In this drill, make ten lay-ups at each end of the court. This means practicing twenty fast breaks. In this process, you are conditioning yourself for the frantic pace of a basketball player.

A simple way for two players to practice passing is simply to pass the ball back and forth to each other. They should make ten chest passes, being sure to follow the fundamentals previously mentioned, then ten bounce passes, ten lob passes, and so on.

Naturally, the shorter a pass, the less the possibility of the ball being intercepted. This makes the short pass ideal for moving the ball. Short, snappy passes are far better than the slow, time-consuming dribbling that hampers an offense.

WHY PASSING IS IMPORTANT

Motion and ball handling are the only way to penetrate a defense effectively. Passing may be compared to the way a car is built on the assembly line in Detroit. The man at the start of the production line, beginning with the shell of the car, is as important as the man who aligns the steering wheel. Just as every man's job is important in the production of the automobile, the passer in the fast break is as important as the player who scores.

The fast break is dynamic and essential to winning, but the simple chest, bounce, one-hand, and two-hand passes must be mastered before the fast break can be executed properly.

PASSING POINTERS

There certainly is more to passing than simply throwing and catching the ball. It is important to know the position of your defender and the other defenders, especially the one guarding your intended receiver. Use peripheral vision to keep track of everyone around you.

Always try to keep your pass away from your receiver's defender. Even if your receiver and his guard were standing 20 feet away from you, you would not throw the ball between the two players. This would be giving them both an equal chance to get the ball. You don't make a pass when there is a fifty-fifty chance that it will not reach its intended destination.

Pass the ball to the side of your receiver that is away from his defender. For instance, if the defender is to the left of your teammate, throw the ball to the right side of your receiver.

Another point to remember is to fake before you pass. Do this frequently. You don't want to telegraph your passes, that is, let the opposition know you are going to pass the ball. If you always pass without faking, or always fake before you pass, the defender will anticipate this. If you fake now and then, you will throw your defender off guard.

A point about getting the ball into the bigman under the basket is worth mentioning. When you have completed a dribble, feed the ball to the center, or bigman, right away, before your defensive man gets set for a play. You can get the ball into the center on any angle. However, the easi-

LESS THAN 50-50. In this situation, if I were to pass the ball to Cazzie Russell (33), there would be little chance that it would ever reach him because the defenders are just too close. The best thing for me to do is wait for a chance to pass to another open receiver or dribble away from the defensive players.

est pass is from the side. This gets the center out of the three-second lane (the area in which no offensive team member can remain for more than three seconds without losing the ball on a violation).

If the bigman is in position for a shot, give him the ball at chest level. A low pass forces the receiver to bend for the ball and then to raise it to shooting level after making the catch. This bending and raising, naturally, requires time and could lead to the shot being blocked. It also causes the shot to be rushed. A pass at chest level makes shooting the ball just a little easier —and that can be the difference between a goal and a miss.

If the receiver is cutting for the basket, the passer should give him the ball at chest level, also. A low pass would make it difficult for him to make the catch since he, undoubtedly, is moving at top speed to break away from his defender.

Now, for the cardinal rule of passing: Never throw a cross-court pass.

The cross-court pass is an open invitation for an interception. It is the pass that most often leads to an unmolested lay-up for the opposition because your team is caught with its defense down. Even if you complete the cross-court pass, in most instances it does not improve the offensive situation, that is, get your team closer to the basket.

It is quite discouraging to see your team work hard for an opportunity to shoot, and then see the opposition make the score because of a stupid mistake such as an intercepted cross-court pass.

RECEIVING A PASS

The receiver must have his eyes on the ball and his hands in a target position. Never keep your hands down, and never stand in one position on the court. Use two hands when catching the ball. Then you can start your shot, dribble, or pass. Your fingers should be comfortably spread and slightly bent. As you receive the ball, your hands should come back toward your body. Do not battle or fight the ball. Be relaxed and give with it.

You can cut down on interceptions by moving toward the ball when there is the slightest chance that a defense man might intercede.

TIPS ON PASSING

- Be able to throw any type of pass.
- Be able to pass one-handers with either hand.
- Pass the ball away from a teammate's guard.
- Pass the ball at a speed the receiver can handle.
- Never throw a cross-court pass.
- Use peripheral vision to keep track of the players around you.
- Give the passer a target.
- Go toward the ball when receiving it.
- Know how and when to use the fast break.

DRIBBLING STYLE...is developed
through years of practice and hard
work, but the most important thing
to remember is to have good control
and don't watch the ball.

chapter 4
DRIBBLING

When Dr. Naismith invented basketball as an indoor sport, it was important to eliminate elements from other sports that could be dangerous on a hardwood court. Basketball rules clearly state that "there shall be no running with the ball." This led to the dribble, the only way a player can move with the ball.

The dribble can be highly effective if used properly. But, it can cause severe damage to the offensive attack if used at the wrong time.

The dribble is used to:

1. Advance the ball on offense.
2. Drive the defensive man.
3. Move in for a close shot.
4. Get the ball out of "tight" areas.
5. Control the ball during stalling periods.

If you ever have seen a soccer game, you know that the players handle the ball with their feet as deftly as a basketball player handles the ball with his hands. The proficient basketball player should be able to dribble and control the ball without even looking at it.

The player who can watch all parts of the floor while dribbling the ball can anticipate defensive maneuvers and keep possession of the ball. But the player who looks at the ball he is dribbling can't follow the maneuvers of his teammates, and he can't watch his defensive man. Watching the ball often can lead to a poor pass that may cost your team possession.

HOW TO DRIBBLE

Always dribble the ball with the hand farthest from your defender. Use your body as a shield to protect the ball from your defender. Bounce the ball quickly with your right or left hand on top, guiding the ball to the floor. Your fingers should be in a semi-spread position with the balls of your fingertips as points of contact.

As in other types of ball handling, the palm of the hand is never used for dribbling. The fingertips give the dribbler the control he needs to handle the ball. The elbow is held in a low position, and the forearm is parallel to the ground. Up-and-

down wrist action, used with the bounce of the ball, creates speed and prevents slapping the ball to the floor. A slapped dribble is slow and bounces back erratically. This, obviously, hinders fast movement of the ball.

The dribbler should be prepared to move either right or left and to bounce the ball with either hand using fingertip control. Dribble the ball at knee level most of the time. Get the hand that is going to dribble the ball below waist level immediately. Dribbling a ball at waist level is considered a high dribble. The only time you can use a high dribble is when your defender is not near. Keep your weight forward, and have your body balanced for movement in any direction. Use your whole body to protect the ball whenever a defender is remotely close to the ball.

PROPER STANCE. In dribbling, keep the ball as low as possible and don't look at it. Keep your head up and use your fingertips to bounce and control the ball. Keep your palms away from the ball.

PROTECT THE BALL! Be prepared to switch the ball from one hand to another if a defender should happen to approach you on the ball side. Always keep your body between the ball and the defender, as I am doing here.

THE DANGER OF A HIGH DRIBBLE

In haste, a player may dribble the ball at waist level. If you've ever bounced a ball, you know that it is easier to dribble it high than low. But the good defender will take the ball away from a high dribbler, no matter how quick he may be.

Bill Bradley of the Knicks, the Princeton All-American who came to the professional league with a half-million dollar contract and a high dribble, doesn't dribble above knee level anymore. Long before Bill Bradley had an opportunity to set up an offensive play, talented defenders like Jerry West, Lennie Wilkens, and Al Attles would take possession of the ball by stealing it off the high dribble. Certainly young players can learn the lesson that Bill Bradley learned long ago: keep the dribble low and avoid steals.

CHANGING DIRECTION

If you can dribble in only one direction, the good defensive player will overshift and overplay you. He will play a half-step or even a full-step ahead of you in the direction you are constantly moving. If you can dribble only to the right, your defender will always be to your right side.

Here is a way that you can move in the opposite direction and fool your defender. Plant your right foot on the floor as if you were going to dribble to the right. Bring the shoulder and arm closest to your defender forward and down to protect the ball. Then, with the speed and power of your right foot, push off to begin going to the left. Shift the ball from your right to your left hand. Change hands from right to left as your defensive player shifts from your right to left side.

CHANGING DIRECTION.
Here I have lured Taylor of the Phoenix Suns to my right side. As he goes for the ball, I move it to my left hand and continue dribbling away from the defender.

CHANGING PACE

Once you have mastered the reverse or crossover and can change directions easily, you are ready to learn the *change of pace* dribble. This dribble is actually very easy but requires split-second movement once the defender is fooled.

Begin by dribbling the ball at a slow speed or tempo. Move toward one of your teammates. This will force your defender to look behind him to see if your teammate's position is going to prevent him from guarding you. As the defender looks to the side and back, start dribbling toward the basket at an accelerated pace. This tactic will give you a little distance on your defender, at least enough to attempt a lay-up if the way is clear.

REVERSE DRIBBLE

The best way to change direction is with the reverse dribble. This dribble is often called the crossover, but to keep things simple we'll refer to it as the reverse. This dribble is used to fool the defender into committing himself to a specific direction so you can drive into the basket.

In reversing from right to left, your right foot hits the floor, and you suddenly shift all of your weight to your left as you shove off with your right foot. This fools your defender into thinking that you are moving to the right. Then, you pick up the dribble with your left hand, protecting the ball with your body. Look for the slightest chance of outdistancing your defender. If you get it, drive for the basket. This often will result in a lay-up, or it will force one of the other defenders to drop off his man to guard you. Then, you can pass to your unguarded teammate, who will have an open shot to the basket.

BEHIND-THE-BACK DRIBBLE

Although the behind-the-back dribble is somewhat fancy, it can be useful if it is not overused. However, because it is difficult, it is not used by most players. You should not even think about using the behind-the-back dribble until you have put control in your dribbling. You are ready for the be-

BEHIND-THE-BACK DRIBBLE. Fingertip control is essential for executing the behind-the-back dribble. Here my left hand is controlling the ball, and my right hand is ready to take over the dribble.

hind-the-back dribble when you can handle the ball with either hand, can look at all of your teammates and defenders without looking at the ball, and can change direction in a fraction of a second.

Long arms and large hands are helpful in the behind-the-back dribble. Keep the ball as low as possible as you begin to transfer it behind your back. With one

UNDER-THE-LEG DRIBBLE. In dribbling the ball between your legs, make sure your hands are in position to push the ball through and to continue the dribble after the ball clears your legs. Your feet should be far enough apart so that the ball can clear your legs easily.

quick movement, flick the ball behind your back. Extend your flicking hand as far as possible to control the ball. As you turn, be prepared to pick up the dribble with your other hand immediately.

UNDER-THE-LEG DRIBBLE

The under-the-leg dribble was not created just to be fancy. If your defender decides to play you tight and goes around you for the ball, bounce the ball under the leg that is farthest from your defender. You must switch your hands quickly. If the ball is pushed under the leg with the right hand, the left hand must be ready to continue control of the ball. The dribbling hand should be as low to the floor as possible. It is easy to change direction using this under-the-leg dribble.

DRIVING

Dribbling is a fundamental that even the shooter, who rarely handles the ball, must know. But the expert dribbler, or ball handler, as he is called, will be able to utilize his skills in a drive for the basket.

You should drive with the ball only when you can clearly beat your defender with a half-step advantage and when the other defenders are not blocking your path to the basket. Do not drive for the sake of driving. The opportunity must be present.

If you are a good outside shooter, meaning you can shoot consistently from 18 feet and more, the defense will be playing you tightly. Whenever your defender is close (within a 3-foot range or less), you have an opportunity to drive. Your shooting reputation lures your defender closer than he might otherwise guard an offensive player. He is looking for your long, outside shot. This gives you a perfect opportunity to go around him.

DRIVING. Here I have an especially good driving opportunity because my teammate
Phil Jackson is blocking my defender, giving me time to go around him toward the basket.

How do you go around him?

By faking.

Hold the ball with both hands, and push it suddenly into the air above your head, so you appear to be shooting. However, don't release the ball; hold it firmly. As the defender goes off his feet into the air to block what he thinks is a shot, go around him, dribbling as fast as you can toward the basket. Another way of faking is to twist your head away from the basket and move your shoulder in the same direction. Do this quickly, luring the defensive player into taking a step away from the basket. Then, dribble the ball toward the basket.

Still another way to fake your defender is by yelling to one of your teammates warning him of a pass. Then, hold the ball firmly, and extend it toward your teammate as if you were going to pass. As the defensive man moves toward you to intercept the pass, dribble the ball the opposite way.

DRIBBLING ADVANTAGES

The fake pass, fake shot, and dribble gives the good ball handler the opportunity to drive. Once a defender is out of position, the other defensive players move in to cover his mistake. This, in turn, means that somewhere on the floor there is an offensive player who is not being guarded and has the opportunity for an open shot. If it is your defensive man who leaves you, race for the basket so that you will be in a position to receive an open pass and shoot.

One rule is important to remember: Never overdribble.

The time you waste by simply bouncing the ball on the floor gives the opposition a chance to organize its defense. By just dribbling and not moving the ball toward the basket, you are accomplishing nothing.

DON'T WASTE THE DRIBBLE

When you take possession of the ball, you can do one of three things: dribble, pass, or shoot. Once you dribble the ball and stop, there are only two possibilities remaining: pass or shoot. At this point, with the knowledge that you have only two possibilities, the defense can adjust itself and play you much tighter. By putting pressure on the ball, the defense can make it difficult for you to pass or shoot. Because of this, don't make the mistake of taking a pass and immediately beginning a dribble without thinking. Once you bounce the ball, you can't dribble again. If you do, a violation called a double dribble or discontinue is called. The penalty for this violation is loss of ball possession.

If you take a pass or rebound and bounce the ball, you may be using up your dribble without getting any value from it. This is a bad habit that you must eliminate from your ball handling techniques. However, it is a habit that many players have—even in the professional ranks.

Tips on Dribbling

- Keep the ball low.
- Protect the ball at all times.
- Stay alert.
- Fake.
- Don't dribble at one speed.
- Don't waste your dribble by bouncing the ball without a purpose.
- Keep your head up to watch the movement of the offensive and defensive players.
- Don't watch the ball.
- Use your fingers, not your palms.
- Be able to use both hands, so you can dribble in any direction.
- Practice.

REBOUNDING...is an important part of winning.
The team that gets the rebound prevents the other
team from getting the ball and scoring...
and after all, that's what the game is all about.

chapter 5
REBOUNDING

The average daily newspaper carries a box score of basketball games showing the goals, free throws, and total points for each player on a team. However, this type of box score hardly tells the whole story. Many newspapers, therefore, carry what is known as the full box score. This not only shows the goals, free throws, and total points, but it also reports the shots taken, the assists, and the rebounds. When the ball comes off the backboard after a missed shot, it is called a rebound.

A look at the rebound total usually provides you with a unique insight into why a team won a game. Notice that the team that takes the most rebounds usually takes the most shots in a game. And the team that has the most rebounds prevents the opposition from shooting.

Everyone notices the points scored in a game and who scored them, but not everyone notices rebounds or the rebounder. The fact is that the rebounder often controls the entire tempo of the game, and rebounding is often a neglected skill. It is, however, one of the most important parts of winning in basketball.

A team without rebounders is a losing one.

HOW TO REBOUND

The first thing to remember in rebounding is to get closer to the basket than your opponent. The closer you are to the basket and the further away your opponent is, the more rebounds you'll get.

After getting an inside position, spread your feet apart with one foot slightly ahead of the other. Keep your body low, back straight, and head up. In this position your opponent should be behind you. As you spread your feet, crouch slightly so you will have some spring in your jump when you go up for the rebound. Throw out your elbows to make it difficult for your opponent to go around you.

Timing the grab is important. You should be at the peak of your jump as the ball is descending from the rim. If the ball is on the rim while you're at the top of your jump, you'll never get the rebound. When you go up for the ball, don't simply flick your fingers at it or bat it. The idea is to grab the ball firmly and securely.

As you gain control of the ball, throw out your legs and spread your arms in a wing-like position so that your opponent can't reach over your body to get the ball. If your opponent does make contact with your body, he will be fouling you.

As soon as you have the ball, pull it down and protect it with your body. Under no circumstances should you attempt to dribble a defensive rebound. Your opponent easily can intercept your dribble, and by being so close to the basket, he would have a perfect opportunity to score.

A quick pass to a teammate would be more desirable than dribbling a rebounded ball. A fake also would be a smart thing to do, since your opponents would not be able to anticipate your next move.

AGGRESSIVENESS

Certainly, positioning for a rebound is primary. But the ball does not find its way to your hands simply because you have the best position. You can follow all the fundamentals of getting rebounds but still be missing one important ingredient: aggressiveness.

Aggressiveness and desire are two of the biggest factors in determining who'll get a rebound. Following the rebounding techniques that I have discussed will help to make you aggressive. Want the ball? Want the rebound? Then go in and get it. Rebounding creates shots; shots create points. Points win games.

AS I GO UP...to take my shot, Willis Reed (19) is moving in for a rebound position. This is an excellent example of how a player anticipates the action of a game so that he is in the best position at the right time.

WHO SHOULD REBOUND?

It is natural to assume that the bigman should be the rebounder most of the time. He should. But this doesn't mean that the other players shouldn't be able to rebound, too. Dave DeBusschere of the Knicks is a classic example of how a smaller man can rebound among the giants of the pro game.

When the Knicks were winning their first championship, every time they needed an important rebound, DeBusschere got it for them. It should be mentioned, however, that Willis Reed positioned himself so that players like Lew Alcindor, Wilt Chamberlain, and Westley Unseld were blocked off the boards, making it possible for DeBusschere to grab the missed shots.

This all goes to prove that you don't have to be an exceptionally tall player to be a good rebounder. More essential are vigorous, aggressive, speedy tactics combined with the basic fundamentals of rebounding.

DEFENSIVE TECHNIQUE

By forming a triangle under the basket, three defensive men can control the backboard. As the shot is taken, one player (usually the tallest) stations himself in the foul lane with one teammate on either side and to the front of him to form a triangle.

The teammates on the right and left of the center player are positioned on the lane lines, almost as if they were readying themselves for a free throw attempt. In this position, the tallest player in the foul lane is directly in front of the rim. However, he never goes under the rim because he would be out of position.

With this triangular setup, the blocked-out offensive team can get very few rebounds. Position is often more important than jumping ability. The jumper doesn't get the rebound in most instances if he is jockeyed to the outside by a smart rebounder.

OFFENSIVE TECHNIQUE

Offensively, you must get around your defensive man and get closer to the basket than he is to pick up the rebound. This is a difficult task, and you must be extremely aggressive.

The player who comes down the floor quickly, before his opponent, has a much better chance of establishing a good rebounding position. Your opponent may try to do the same thing to you, so speed is essential. If your opponent has the better position, you can move in to his left or right when he looks up toward the basket as a shot is taken.

Go to the boards whenever a shot is taken. Even if the ball is shot from the other side of the court, race toward the backboard. This is called crashing the board and should be done by every frontcourt player on the offensive team, not just the taller ones.

As I have mentioned previously, basketball has changed so that there is no such thing as a center, two forwards, and two guards. The backcourt player may be positioned in one of the corners as a play develops, and the frontcourt player may be in the backcourt area when a shot is attempted. When a shot is taken, the player in the frontcourt should go to the boards; the player in the backcourt should drop back into a defensive position so that he can prevent the opposition from developing a fast break.

STEALING REBOUNDS

If your opponent rebounds according to the fundamental rules—keeping his arms, elbows, and legs extended after he has control of the ball—you will not be able to steal too many rebounds. However, if he does not protect the ball with his body after he gets the rebound, you will have a good chance to steal.

As your opponent is bringing the ball down from the rebound and while it is over his head, reach in and hook the ball away from him. If your opponent has both hands on the ball, you can try to slap it out of his grasp. Of course, this is even easier if he only has one hand on the ball. Reach in for the ball when your opponent makes the mistake of bringing it to one side of his body without using his arms and elbows to protect it from your defensive attack.

If the rebounder dribbles the ball, slap it away from him toward one of your teammates. If he is not an extremely competent dribbler, simply steal the ball away from him and look for either a shot or another good offensive situation. If the rebounder has a habit of passing the ball to his team's playmaker every time he takes a defensive rebound, anticipate this pass so you can steal the ball. If the ball can't be stolen, then make it difficult for the playmaker to move with the ball.

DOUBLY GOOD. Although I am trying mainly to block the shot of my opponent here, I also am in the best position to get the rebound after the player makes the shot.

TIPS ON REBOUNDING

- Establish your position close to the basket and in front of your opponent.

- Block out your opponent at every opportunity.

- Stay out of the area underneath the basket. You must be in front of the rim to take a rebound.

- Crash the boards whenever you are in a frontcourt spot and a shot is attempted.

- Jump as high as you can for a rebound.

- Time your jump so that you are at your maximum height as the ball is on its downward flight.

- Catch the ball with two hands; one hand on top and the other underneath so you won't lose possession.

- Protect rebounds with your entire body.

- Be aggressive and alert at all times.

IN DEFENSING...your man, you don't have to be right up on top of him to do a good job. Just keep your eye on the ball, as I'm doing here, and force the dribbler to move in the direction you want him to go.

chapter 6
INDIVIDUAL DEFENSE

Bill Russell made defense glamorous by blocking shots and intimidating shooters. When Willis Reed came into the league, I remember that he was afraid to shoot against Russell. Bearded Bill would block so many shots that the Knicks' offense would come apart. Defense won championships for Boston for many years. And, of course, defense helped the Knicks win a championship, too. Whenever I think about how the Knicks won their championship title, I hear the 19,500 Madison Square Garden fans yelling: "Dee-fense. Dee-fense."

The modern basketball player must have an assortment of skills. And one of them is defense. Give a boy a football and he wants to throw a pass. Try to start a baseball game and everyone wants to be either the batter or pitcher. Most young players don't think of football as more than touchdowns and field goals, or of baseball as more than pitching and hitting, or of basketball as more than shooting.

In winning a game, defense is almost as important as scoring, despite the fact that the scorers receive most of the publicity.

Red Holzman explains the Knicks' victories by saying: "The defense makes the offense." You can see this, especially, when an interception leads to an easy basket, or when a good defensive player breaks down the other team's offensive patterns. A player must be well-rounded, and this means being able to play defense as well as offense.

If you are having difficulty shooting, you should not allow this to affect your defensive performance. Defense is aggressiveness and desire. It is also savvy, knowledge, moxie, skill, or whatever word you want to call it when you are able to contain the other team.

To play good defense doesn't mean that you are going to prevent your man from scoring all the time. But it does mean that you can stop a lot of the shots that he otherwise would make.

And this really is not difficult if you know the fundamentals of good defense and can apply them to any defensive situation. Basically, though, defense is a simple assignment: Prevent your man from getting the ball, and he can't score.

DEFENSIVE STANCE. Spread your feet apart and stagger them
so that you can move easily and quickly in any direction. Put one hand
up to prevent a shot and the other hand down to prevent a pass.
Of course, you must switch your hands from up to down and down to up
as the ball is moved from one side to the other.

STANCE

When guarding an opponent use the proper defensive stance whenever your man has the ball. The following tips should help you develop the proper defensive stance:

1. Keep one foot back, feet staggered, so that you can change direction in a split second.
2. Keep your weight on the balls of your feet but back so that you have complete control and mobility.
3. Extend one hand into the air to block the shooter's vision and generally to distract him. This hand also should be used to block passes and shots.
4. Position the other hand at waist level. This hand is used to drive the opponent away. It can block a shot taken by a poor shooter from hip level. More importantly, it can block a pass or be used to hamper the offensive player's dribbling.
5. When your opponent is not a good shooter, keep both hands down low with the palms out (two-hand-down defense) and your eyes focused on his midsection. In this position, you can protect against passes and force dribbling mistakes.

6. Look directly at your opponent; always keep your head up.

In addition to being alert at all times, the good defensive player is always between his man and the basket. If the offensive man does wedge in between you and the basket, his team has the advantage that leads to the so-called "percentage shots," which generally result in scores. One of the most important things in defensive positioning is keeping your feet staggered. If your feet are on an even line, your opponent can go around you easily because you won't be able to move fast enough.

VISION AND VOICE

It is essential for a defensive player to keep his head up so he can see. Looking down on the floor or trying to keep an eye on the ball can destroy good defense. Use your peripheral vision to see what is going on on all sides.

A good defensive player uses his eyes to keep in touch with what's happening, and he also uses his voice to warn and alert his teammates of any changes in defensive movement. Don't be afraid to shout a command to your teammate. If your team loses possession yell: "Back, back." If you gain control of the ball on a steal, yell: "Ball, ball," and move down the court quickly.

Work out a system of word symbols with your teammates so the other team won't anticipate your moves by your voice commands.

DEFENSING SCREENS

If one of your opponent's players runs between you and the man you are guarding (screening), make the following adjustment:

If the screening player is to your left, take a long step with right foot and spin toward the player who has blocked you. As you spin, go into a semi-crouch position with your knees bent and your feet spread wide apart. One foot should be back and the other extended forward. Have your weight on the balls of your feet, and have your head up to see what is going on. Keep your head bent slightly forward so that you can move quickly in any direction. Always look to both sides, but *never turn your head* to look at the ball.

If you turn your head, your opponent will use that split second to go around you to the basket. By the time you look again, your opponent will be under the basket, probably taking his shot.

FORCING THE BALL

In defense, the offensive dribbler is forced to move the ball away from his opponent's hand, which is extended downward. Thus, you can force the ball in any direction you like by just moving your hand toward the ball.

If you are playing near the sideline or end line, it is usually best to drive the dribbler toward the center of the floor where your teammates will be able to help you defend. If an offensive player is driving toward the end line, keep him from going around you on the outside. If he goes around you on the inside, toward the middle of the court, one of your teammates should be able to help you. However, if he goes around you on the outside, your teammates can't move in fast enough to assist.

In general, defense that works results when the defensive player makes the first move. After you decide the direction in which you want to force the offensive player, take your first step with your foot going in that direction. Then bring the other foot into position, somewhat like a boxer when he is moving toward his opponent. As you

FORCING THE BALL. Here the offensive dribbler has had to move the ball from his left to his right hand to keep it away from my defending advance. In situations like this, I always try to keep the player away from the basket and move him toward one of my teammates or toward a position where he is forced to make an awkward shot.

practice moving in this crablike fashion, you will get the feel of it. Work on this move by runnng a back-up drill down the entire court a couple of times a day. By using this method you will be able to force your man to move in the direction you want him to go.

STEALING THE BALL

Whenever you attempt to steal the ball, you must be reasonably certain that you can get possession. A miss gives the offensive team a fantastic advantage because your teammates, in anticipation of a steal, already have switched their positions to start on an offensive charge. They don't expect to be on the defense. A steal, however, gives you the opportunity for a lay-up in most instances.

To make a steal, you must watch the general pattern that a player uses in handling the ball. Some players bounce the ball as soon as they receive it; others bounce it two or three times and then make a pass; still others always start to dribble with their right hand.

To help you develop the skill of recognizing offensive ball-handling patterns, ask yourself some of the following questions:

1. Does my opponent always dribble the ball with the same hand?
2. Does he dribble at the same pace?
3. Is a pass generally made at a certain spot on the floor?
4. Does the same player usually receive the pass at this particular spot?
5. Does the player receiving the pass immediately protect the ball?
6. Is the ball usually brought down the center of the court or down one of the sides?
7. Is there a player on the other team who has difficulty dribbling the ball?
8. Does my opponent like to shoot the ball after bouncing it once or twice?
9. Is there any hesitation about deciding what to do with the ball once it is received?

If you think you've found a pattern to the offensive team's play, you have a good chance of making a steal. Of course, you have to react quickly and instinctively. Lunging at the ball (throwing all your weight forward), is an outright gamble because it throws you off balance and makes it impossible for you to get at the ball. In the steal, your hands are positioned with one hand up and one hand at waist level. Your arms and hands move in to take the ball. Your feet immediately start you on a course toward the basket or another teammate.

USING THE FAKE

In guarding against a shot, it should be remembered that the offensive player will give you a fake. He can fake you with his head, with his eyes, shoulders, hands, and feet. But he can't fake you with his waist. Wherever his waist goes, so goes the ball.

As a defensive player, you also can use the fake. If you use your shoulder to fake, the offensive player will react, defensively, to protect the ball. This maneuver cuts down on his offensive momentum because your opponent is more concerned with keeping the ball away from you than with making a shot.

AVOIDING FOULS

Games are won or lost on fouling. Coaches spend time teaching plays aimed at making one particular player on a team foul out. Run this play enough, and it is likely that this player will leave the game. Obviously, if this player is the best shooter on the team, it is likely that the team will lose.

Every player must know how to avoid fouling. Because it is natural to bring the arm downward after attempting to block a shot, fouls often result unintentionally. Even if a player misses his shot, if he's fouled while shooting, he gets two chances to make a shot at the free throw line.

In going up to block a shot, avoid a hacking motion. Instead, make a defensive motion up where the shot is taken. Keep your hand up to block the shot, and don't bring it down even when the shot is actually released. If your hand comes down, there is a chance that the referee may call a foul on you by mistake. When your hand is up in the air, it's not likely that you'll foul someone or have a foul called on you by mistake; also, you are in a good position to rebound missed shots.

STOPPING THE PIVOTMAN

Certainly, there isn't any way to stop a Wilt Chamberlain from scoring, and there isn't much even Wilt Chamberlain can do to prevent Willis Reed from making a 30-foot one-hand shot while fading away from the basket. But the non-professional player will not be confronted with this type of player in 999 out of 1000 games.

In defensing a pivotman, follow these rules:

1. Stay in front of your man when he is playing close to the basket. There is no point in playing behind him, because if he gets the ball, there is virtually no way to prevent him from making a shot.
2. Beat the bigman to his spot. Many pivot players shoot from a favorite spot on the floor. Beat him to that spot, and he is at a disadvantage. Force him to make the plays he does not want to make.
3. If the pivot player is a good right-handed shooter, overplay him by a half or even full step to the right. Conversely, follow the opposite procedure for the good left-handed pivot shooter.
4. Don't allow the pivot player to move freely underneath the boards. Compete for rebounds, and keep your hands up to block shots.

STAY IN FRONT OF YOUR MAN. When the man you are defending is in the vicinity of the basket, stay in front of him or between him and the basket. Here I block a pass made by one of the Phoenix Suns. Notice that I am standing just far enough away from my man to make it more difficult for him to pass over me.

TIPS ON INDIVIDUAL DEFENSE

- Adjust to situations—slide, switch, and move.
- Always watch your opponent's chest, not his eyes, head, feet, or arms.
- Don't turn your head to watch the ball.
- Use peripheral vision.
- Always keep your feet in the "staggered" defensive stance.
- Never cross your feet.
- Use a boxer's step to move laterally.
- Keep one hand up and the other down and out.
- Don't be afraid to talk on defense.
- When screened, know how to roll defensively.
- Never allow more than one man between you and your opponent.
- In stealing the ball, make sure you can take possession. Don't lunge.
- Always keep yourself between the opponent and the basket.
- Overshift or overplay when necessary.
- Always be alert.

TEAM DEFENSE...relies entirely on team cooperation. Here I am working with Walt Frazier (10) in setting up a defensive play to stop one of the Phoenix Suns from passing the ball to one of his teammates.

chapter 7
TEAM DEFENSE

Defense is not just an individual thing.

If your man slips away from you and one of your teammates makes a shift and switches to your man, your team is playing good defense. However, if your teammate doesn't switch, he is just as much at fault as you are for letting your man get away. This game is a five-man effort, and defense must be played by the whole team if it is to be successful.

Even when you play man-for-man defense (when each man on the defensive team guards one member of the offensive team), there will be some double-teaming. In today's game, the idea is to keep pressure on the ball, that is, make it difficult for the player with the ball to pass or dribble. And, certainly, you don't want him to score.

A good defensive team follows certain fundamentals:

1. Allow an opponent who is weak in ball handling to dribble or pass when he is outside of the scoring area. He probably will make a mistake in trying to move the ball off to another teammate, giving your team a chance for an interception. However, don't allow him to handle the ball so easily when he has a chance to score.

2. If the opposition has a good bigman, or pivotman, force the ball to the sidelines as much as possible. Allow the opposition's guards to over dribble and clog the middle of the court, making it difficult for the bigman to obtain possession of the ball.

3. If a player likes to shoot from a certain section of the floor, defense that section before the offensive player has a chance to position himself.

4. If the opposition has a player who can drive well, defend in such a manner as to draw charging fouls. That is, place yourself so that you have established your floor position a full step ahead of your opponent. Then, when he gets the ball and wheels around to drive toward the basket, he'll run right into you. When contact is made, fall flat on your back. The referee will call charging.

5. Use pressing defenses whenever possible. Prevent the ball from being driven down the court quickly. If a player has difficulty passing, the ball moves slowly. And, of course, passes made in haste are intercepted.

6. Rebounding is part of defense. Whenever the opposition attempts a shot, be in a position to try for the rebound. Get the rebound so the other team won't have another chance for a score.

ZONE DEFENSE

In zone defense, men are assigned to defend certain areas of the court rather than a player on the other team (man-for-man defense). Where the defensive man positions himself within his zone depends upon where the ball is at the time. There are many types of zone defenses, that is, there are many ways that the court area around the basket being defended can be distributed among the defensive players.

In the 2-1-2 zone defense (Diagram 4), one man is positioned in front of the basket just below the top of the keyhole (circular area at the top of the free-throw lane). Two players are positioned in front and to the right and left of him outside of the free-throw lane. The other two players are stationed under the board, to the left and right of the free-throw lane.

In the 1-2-2 zone defense, again one man is positioned in front of the basket in the free-throw lane, but instead of being toward the top of the keyhole, as in the 2-1-2 zone, he is more toward the center. The other four players in the 1-2-2 zone defense

DIAGRAM 4. 2-1-2 zone defense.

are in approximately the same position as in the 2-1-2. However, the two players near the boards move up so that they are only slightly ahead of the man in front of the basket.

The only difference between the 2-1-2 zone defense and the 2-2-1 is that the player in front of the basket moves up to the very top of the keyhole, and the two front players move back toward the basket, standing on the outer edges of the free-throw lane.

In the 1-3-1 zone defense (Diagram 5), three players are in the free-throw lane. One player is in the top of the keyhole, the second is just below the foul line, and the third player is at the bottom of the free-throw lane directly under the basket. The remaining two defensive players stand out-side of the free-throw lane to the left and right of the center player.

As the offensive team approaches, the defense shifts to keep the area impenetrable as the ball is moved around the periphery of the zone. This forces the offensive team to shoot from outside the zone, where generally there is less accuracy. Also, by maintaining a strong zone even after the ball is shot, the defensive team is grouped around the basket to grab rebounds of missed shots.

Your coach will decide the type of zone to be used against the opposition. After studying a team on various occasions, the coach can pinpoint its weaknesses. So he will adjust the zone defense in such a way as to force the opposition to shoot from their weak areas.

DIAGRAM 5. 1-3-1 zone defense.

A BIG WEAK SPOT

Now that you've seen how the zone defense works, you probably have already spotted some of its weaknesses.

The biggest weakness, however, is the fact that many shooters can and do penetrate the zone defense. In pro ball, there are few weak shooters. It is nothing for a player to shoot from 30 feet away. Competent amateur players also can shoot from this distance. Consequently, the zone defense has little success against an offense that can simply shoot over it.

Even the smartest coaches leave holes in their zone defenses. That's why zone defenses give me the best opportunities for open shots. Remember, the zone defense is only as effective as the opposition is ineffective. Therefore, do not wander from your position in the zone. Play your area tenaciously and aggressively, and pressure the ball.

Zone defense is one kind of team defense. However, I feel that the young player should spend little time on it at the outset and instead should master man-for-man defense.

MAN-FOR-MAN

Just about anyone can defend a portion of the floor, but not everyone can defend a good offensive player.

In the man-for-man defense, each player must learn to assume complete responsibility for an opposing player. Individual defensive fundamentals must be employed to their fullest; the defense has to force the opposition to change its tactics.

Use the fundamentals you learned in the chapter on individual defense to implement man-for-man defense on the team level. Select a man to guard who is similar to you in stature and speed. Keep this man unless there is a switching situation. You can also change your man during a jump ball in order to cover the jumper's man. One other time that the man-for-man defense changes is during a fast break.

STOPPING THE FAST BREAK

In basketball today, just about every team uses the fast break at some time during a game. Therefore, your team must know how to stop it. For every offensive move there is a defensive move—move and countermove:

1. Stop the fast break at its inception. If your team can control offensive rebounding and keep the ball from being stolen or intercepted, this helps to stop the fast break.
2. Stop the first pass. Look to see where the playmaker of the other team stations himself. He is the one who gets the first pass from the rebounder. If you can't intercept this pass, make it impossible for the playmaker to move the ball quickly downcourt in an effort to run a fast break. If you can stop this playmaker, you usually can stop the fast break. And, of course, if you make some interceptions, it's likely that you will score some easy points.
3. Stop the dribbler. If your team can tie up the dribbler or force him to stop dribbling and advancing the ball, you can stop the momentum of the opposition's fast break. Keep your hands parallel to the floor with the palms out, and force the dribbler to advance the way you want him to. If you can't stop the dribbler, head back at full speed to protect your basket, and group to keep the dribbler on the outside of your defense, away from the basket. (Here, you

have a combination of a man-for-man and a zone defense.) But be careful of the good, long-distance shooters.

4. Doubleteam the ball whenever possible. This means that one of your teammates should move in to help you defense the player with the ball. This makes it *doubly* hard for the offensive player to dribble, pass, or shoot because there are four hands ready to make an interception instead of the usual two.

KNOCK OFF THE PIVOTMAN

The pivotman is the player who most often gets the rebounds for the offense. He is the one you have to stop to halt the fast break. The following are some special ways to help stop the bigman:

1. Use a semi-zone defense. That is, have one of your teammates help you surround the pivotman to prevent him from gaining possession.

2. Get the pivot player into foul trouble. Whenever the center gets some early fouls, it might be a good idea to flow some of your offensive plays at him, forcing him into those situations where he usually draws fouls.

3. Use the jam-up tactic. Prevent the pivotman from getting near the basket by jamming up the center of the court with defensive players.

CLOSE TO THE BASKET

Never attempt a tight man-for-man defense close to the basket because there are too many well-planned offenses designed to penetrate this kind of defense. Defensive players should be free to move in and help one another when their own offensive man is poorly positioned.

DIAGRAM 6. Man-for-man defense close to the basket.

If the ball is passed into the three-second zone, the shooter can be charged by all five men. However, this is not wise because he may pass the ball to one of his outlying teammates, who then would have a clear shot to the basket. The defensive players should move into the ball but at the same time be flexible enough to cut off the passing path to the free players.

In Diagram 6, the offensive man, O_1, has the ball near the basket, while X_1 defenses him. The ball is passed to O_3; X_4 drops back to cover X_5's man or to rebound. X_5 doubles up on O_3 and also can protect the basket area. X_3 moves toward O_5. X_2 moves up to the ball, ready to pick up any loose player. X_1 retreats to what he thinks will be the line of the pass. He is ready to intercept the pass or to rebound.

DIAGRAM 7. Defense against out-of-bounds play.

OUT-OF-BOUNDS PLAYS

When a ball is being thrown inbounds, you can use a five-on-four defense. In Diagram 7, X_1 has dropped off O_1, the man throwing the ball in. X_2 and X_3 are playing the ball and their man. X_4 and X_5 are in front of their men, but standing a few feet away to intercept the ball if it is passed to either O_4 or O_5.

There is no need to guard the man with the ball because most offensive players ask their own teammates to stand back on throw-ins to give them room to maneuver. X_1 is the only defensive player not fronting his man. He is playing off the man throwing the ball inbounds. His assignment is to play a zone in that area and pick up any offensive man moving in the direction of the ball.

TIPS ON TEAM DEFENSE

- Defense is a team effort.
- Allow a poor ball handler to pass or dribble outside of the scoring area.
- Force the ball to the sidelines when the offense has a good pivotman.
- Defense a favorite offensive shooting position by getting there first.
- Defend a good driving offensive man by forcing him into a situation where he will draw a charging foul.
- Press the offense.
- Get those rebounds.
- Zone defense is only as effective as the opposition is ineffective.
- Stop the fast break by stopping the first pass, stopping the dribbler, and double teaming.
- Stop the pivotman by using a semi-zone defense, getting the bigman into foul trouble, and using the jam-up tactic.
- Never attempt a tight man-for-man defense close to the basket.

TEAM OFFENSE. Team cooperation is just as important on offense as it is on defense. Here Walt Frazier (10) screens for me so that I can move the ball toward the basket.

chapter 8
TEAM OFFENSE

Individual development is the key to all team play. Master the fundamentals and you are well on your way to building a strong offense. In previous chapters, we have discussed individual techniques such as shooting, passing, dribbling, and rebounding. After you have developed these skills, your team can put together a good offense through timing, coordination, and a few well-executed plays.

Timing and coordination come with practice. During passing drills, for example, you and your teammates should constantly pass the ball as you run, turn, and go through the plays and maneuvers that you've developed to use against your opponents. Master your own style, using discipline and practice as a framework.

There are three types of plays to master to build a solid offense. These are: out-of-bounds plays (from the sidelines and under the basket), jump ball plays, and plays against the man-for-man and zone presses.

OUT-OF-BOUNDS PLAY

In the first out-of-bounds play (Diagram 8), X_1 has been assigned to throw in the ball from under the basket. As X_1 takes possession from the referee, X_2 runs toward the endline to the left of the basket as if he were going to take the pass. However, he actually is creating a screen for X_4, who cuts in to take the ball from X_1. The player guarding X_4, O_4, is blocked by X_2. This gives X_4 an open shot, 10 feet from the basket.

A slightly different out-of-bounds play is shown in Diagram 9. This time, before X_1 passes the ball, he fakes to the outside corner, then makes the pass directly under the basket to X_2, who has an excellent opportunity to make a lay-up. X_4 and X_3 move to clear out the lane for X_2, who must move quickly to beat his defenders, O_2 and O_1 before they block his open shot to the basket.

DIAGRAM 8. First out-of-bounds play.

DIAGRAM 9. Second out-of-bounds play.

In the out-of-bounds play from the side-lines (Diagram 10), X_2, the center, breaks upcourt and receives a pass from X_1, who is throwing in from out-of-bounds. X_3 has moved up to set a screen on O_1. After passing to X_2, X_1 cuts quickly toward the basket. X_2 gives X_1 a return pass, giving X_1 a clear path to the basket.

In Diagram 11, X_1 makes an inbound pass directly under the basket to X_4, who delays for a moment to give X_2 and X_3 a chance to clear out the free-throw lane. X_4's quick move toward the basket creates an open shot. X_4 must fake O_4, throwing him off by least a half step to make the basket without being blocked.

In the fifth out-of-bounds play (Diagram 12) X_1 makes an inbound pass to X_3, who has cut across the free-throw lane to come behind a screen created by X_2. The screen prevents O_3 from blocking X_3's short jump shot.

DIAGRAM 10. Third out-of-bounds play.

DIAGRAM 11. Fourth out-of-bounds play.

DIAGRAM 12. Fifth out-of-bounds play.

JUMP-BALL PLAYS

In the first offensive jump (Diagram 13) the players alternate their positions with a defensive player. The object of the play is to tap the ball to one of the two teammates closest to the basket, X_4 or X_3. When the ball is tapped, in this case to X_4, both X_4 and X_3 move toward the basket. Then X_4 passes the ball to X_3, who makes the shot. When it is difficult for the offensive players to get the proper alternating position on the circle for the jump (Diagram 14), the jumper taps the ball to any one of his players on the side closest to the basket, in this case X_4. Meanwhile X_3 screens for X_1, who breaks for the basket to receive a pass from X_4 and takes the shot.

DIAGRAM 13. Jump ball play.

DIAGRAM 14. Jump ball play.

PENETRATING THE ZONE DEFENSE

When your team gets the ball, the first objective is to move it incourt toward the basket before the defensive zone can be set up. The second objective is to know what kind of zone press the opposition is using. The best pass against the zone defense is an accurate baseball pass. Well-executed long-distance passing does more to disintegrate a zone than any other maneuver.

Quick movement of the ball eventually will create an opening on either the left or right side of a zone defense. In Diagram 15, the defensive zone has shifted to the left, following the ball in X_2's possession.

X_2 passes the ball to X_4, who fakes a lay-up and passes the ball to X_5, who then has an open shot to the basket. Reverse the play for the right-sided defense.

Against a 1-3-1 zone defense, Diagram 16, X_5 has the ball. X_1 shifts to the left or right depending on where X_5 moves the ball. If X_1 is open, the ball is passed to him for the shot. X_2 is open for a shot whenever the zone defense moves too far to the right. Conversely, X_4 is open when the defensive play moves too far to the left. And if the defense moves too far from the center, X_3 will be open at the foul line for a 15-foot shot. The primary function of X_5 is to move the ball quickly and to confuse the defense.

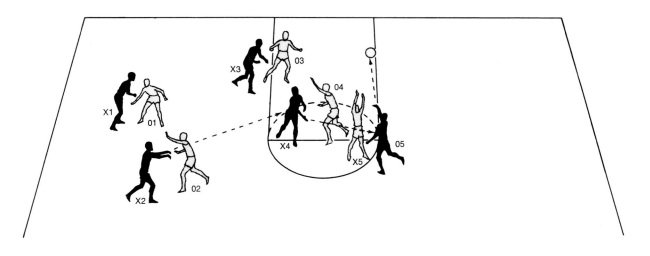

DIAGRAM 15. Penetrating the zone defense.

DIAGRAM 16. Offense against a 1-3-1 zone defense.

MAN-FOR-MAN OFFENSE

To create an easy, open shot, player X_2 in Diagram 17 moves across the free-throw lane and forms a screen to block O_1. His defensive man, O_2, moves with him. This leaves player X_1 free to receive a pass from X_4 as he cuts toward the basket. X_1 has a chance for an easy lay-up from under the basket. This play can be run in reverse, making X_3 the shooter. In this case, X_2 would be positioned on the left side of the free-throw lane and would crossover to the right to block O_3. Then X_5, the player with the ball in this play, would cut toward the basket and pass the ball to X_3 for the lay-up.

To clear out play under the basket (Diagram 18), X_5 has moved the ball to the right side of the court. X_3 and X_4 move with him. Then, X_5 quickly passes the ball to X_2, who in turn passes it to X_1, who then dribbles around O_1 and takes a lay-up shot. This play is called a clear out because all the players on the offensive team cleared out of a specific area so that X_1 would have a good chance for a shot close to the basket.

DIAGRAM 17. Man-for-man offense to create an open shot.

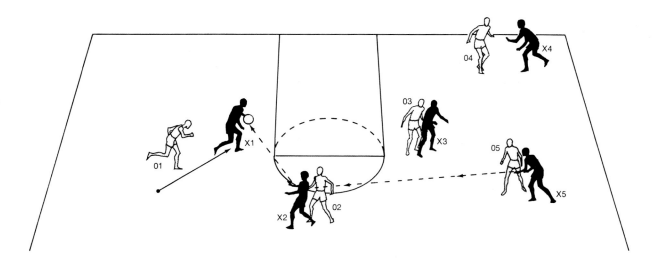

DIAGRAM 18. Man-for-man offense to clear out play under the basket.

STRATEGY

In baseball, the pitcher has a certain job to do and so does the catcher. All of the players have a specific position. The same is true in many other sports. However, this is not true of basketball as it is played today.

The specific position that a player is assigned—forward, center, or guard—is relatively unimportant. Each player must be able to play all positions. Using position terminology and adhering to the strict meaning of words such as forward and guard is passé.

If one player on a team is stopped by the defense, then the other four must provide a larger share of the points. However, the player who is being checked by the defense, certainly, is not out of the game. He still can help his team's offense by creating blocks, rebounding, and passing. Sooner or later, he'll get his shooting opportunities.

The successful offensive team coordinates the actions of five players into various patterns, some of which have been discussed in this chapter. The patterns that a coach uses depend on the strength and size of his players, their quickness and ball-handling abilities, plus, to some extent, the opposition's ability.

The functions of an offense are to obtain a variety of successful shots from the basic patterns of play, to maintain adequate coverage for rebounds, and to take proper defensive measures. The primary offensive players must confuse the defense to immobilize it, while the other teammates must use deploying tactics to distract their opponents from the focal point of attack.

The following factors are essential for a good offense:

1. Each player must understand his function in relation to the others and must know what is required of each of the other four players in a given situation.

2. The team must make smooth transitions from one phase of offense to another and must coordinate ball and player movement.

3. The team should be divided so there are three offensive rebounders, one player who is half rebounder and half defense man, and one who, at all times, is moving back to play defense.

THE FINAL RESULT. If a team employs all of its offensive skills and know-how and adds the extra element of cooperation, it should get this kind of shooting opportunity on every play.

TIPS ON TEAM OFFENSE

- Individual development is the key to all successful team play.

- Team offense comes with timing, coordination, and a few well-executed plays.

- Practice the three types of offensive plays: (1) out-of-bounds plays (from the side and from under the basket); (2) jump ball plays; and (3) plays against the man-for-man and zone presses.

- In penetrating a zone defense, the most important thing to remember is to pass or dribble the ball as quickly as possible.

- The functions of an offense are to obtain a variety of successful shots from the basic play pattern, to maintain adequate coverage for rebounds, and to take proper defensive measures.

- Each player must understand his function in relation to the other team-mates.

- The team must make smooth transitions from one phase of offense to another.

THE DEMANDS OF BASKETBALL...
put a good deal of strain on
your entire physical system,
so it is important that you
work constantly to keep your
body in top physical condition.

chapter 9
CONDITIONING

Basketball is a nonstop game, and it is essential that you be in top physical condition. A basketball player must go up and down the court at racehorse speed and must be prepared to play the entire game. All of this leads, obviously, to the fact that the basketball player must take good care of his body.

FOOD AND LIQUIDS

Watch the kind of food you are eating. Never eat any sweets or desserts during the basketball season, and limit yourself closely during the off-season. Why hinder your body with excess weight?

As a basketball player, I always have followed my same "secret" diet. I have fruit or fruit juice for breakfast along with eggs and buttered rye toast, and, of course, milk. For lunch, I have a sandwich with a raw vegetable, perhaps some soup, and milk or tea. For dinner, I have a high-protein meat, a green vegetable, salad, and a potato. On game days, eat your main meal three and a half to four hours before game time. Salt needs to be replaced daily, particularly during periods of changing climate and temperature. During hot weather, you should take one teaspoon of salt (or salt tablets if you prefer) to six quarts of liquid.

An athlete should drink three to four ounces of saline solution after practicing or playing a game. Taking salt with plenty of liquid prevents gastrointestinal disturbances and improves your ability to perform.

Tea is also an excellent liquid refreshment because it doesn't add excess weight. Cazzie Russell of the Knicks drinks tea spiked with honey. The honey gives him energy and, at the same time, doesn't add the excess weight that is accumulated by eating other sweets.

OVEREXERTION

Never take chances by pushing your body too far. If you play ball in extremely warm weather, heat exhaustion is possible. The recognizable symptoms of heat exhaustion are: nausea, unusual awkwardness, unco-ordinated gait, dizziness, fatigue, indifference, reduced morale, and a rapid, weak pulse rate.

Fortunately, recovery from heat exhaustion is generally rapid and without ill effects, provided there are no complications such as dehydration and salt deficiency. In treating heat exhaustion, have the player lie down in the shade or other comfortable environment out of the sun and drink salted fluids.

Naturally, professional players won't have the problems that the young player, who plays both indoors and outdoors, might encounter. Pro teams employ full-time trainers to look after the bodies of their highly paid athletes. The trainers tape ankles, exercise muscles, and generally mother every player who needs it before a game. And, of course, the conscientious player keeps himself in good shape without being nagged.

EXERCISES

Here are a few simple exercises that will help a player maintain good body condition:

1. Stretch your legs, hips, and lower back by bending and touching the floor with your fingers while keeping your knees straight.
2. Stretch your hamstring muscles by extending your right foot behind your body and bending, touching the floor with your right hand.
3. Build up your thigh and arm muscles by lifting your legs in a drum major strut with your upper trunk leaning back as far as possible. Overemphasize the action of your legs and arms, and pump vigorously. This exercise also will develop your knees and improve your rhythm.
4. Another good exercise is the hip rotation. Kick one leg out and upward as high as your head while keeping the other leg on the floor. Now switch legs quickly, throwing

the leg that had been on the floor into the air as high as possible. Swing each leg in a smooth, relaxed arc, and extend it to maximum height each time.
5. An isometric indoor exercise that is good for building up muscles is to lean against a wall at a 45° angle. Push hard against the wall, exerting as much pressure as you can. When you're at home, go into the kitchen and put your hands under the sink. Try to lift up the sink for about fifteen seconds, exerting all of your arm strength. Do this fifty times a day, and you will find that you're developing your muscle strength.

For a basketball player, these isometric drills are far superior to weightlifting. Weightlifting throws off your shooting touch. You'll be shooting the ball over the backboard instead of scoring. Don't do any weightlifting during the basketball season. Use the kitchen sink and isometrics.

Of course, you should also skip rope and do sit-ups and push-ups to develop a strong body that will endure until the end of the game. In fact, more demands are placed on your shooting and defending skills at the end of the game because of the time aspect.

RUNNING SPEED

After you have finished exercising, work on improving your running speed. In sprinting, the first step is explosive. When you have the ball, this step can be the one that frees you for an easy shot. In defending, this step can make a difference in keeping your opponent under control.

Keep your toes straight ahead of you, and extend your rear running leg to form a straight line from the hip to the toe. To get this extension, strengthen your calf muscle by using isometric exercises or the drum major strut, described previously.

In running, keep your shoulders square. Don't let your arms, shoulders, or hips rotate. Relax your fingers and hands as you run; tight fists slow you down. For this reason, never keep your fingers together while you're playing.

Wind sprints are a must for endurance and will help you to improve your speed. If you are not born with blinding speed, the only way to improve your quickness is to go out and run every day. A basketball player never stops running and moving, so learn how to run.

Breathing must be normal at all times. The neck should remain relaxed, and the eyes should be focused straight ahead, never on the ball. Any attempt to look over your shoulder will shorten your stride and make you lose speed.

A STRONG BODY HELPED ME

I've only been stopped once during my career. It happened a few years ago at the old Madison Square Garden. I was coming down the floor on a fast break, and something tore just above my ankle. While I was lying on the floor, there were pains in my entire leg. To comfort me, the referee, Manny Sokol, called a three-second violation on me. This was one of the few times I was ever called for this violation. I can still laugh over the circumstances because it wasn't the end of my career, as some people thought.

The late Dr. Kazuo Yanagisawa, the Knicks' team physician, operated and sewed together the Achilles tendon that had been torn and braced it with an artificial tendon. Now, I think I have greater strength in the injured leg than in the other one.

However, I owe my successful recovery to my well-conditioned body. There was no flab to prevent healing. During the summer, I ran in the sand out on the beach in Los Angeles. I did the exercises described in this chapter in preparation for the next season. I was able to continue my career because I had kept myself in good condition.

TIPS ON CONDITIONING

- Your body must be in good condition to endure the entire game.
- Eat a well-balanced diet.
- Never eat sweets during the season, and limit your intake of them during the off-season.
- Replace salt in your body after playing or practicing to avoid heat exhaustion.
- Exercise regularly.
- Use isometric exercises rather than weightlifting, which can ruin your shooting touch.
- Develop fast sprinting speed.
- In running, keep your shoulders square, and relax your hands and fingers.
- Try to breathe normally at all times.
- Take good care of your body.

appendix

Write to any one of the following places for a basketball rule book:

ELEMENTARY AND HIGH SCHOOL

National Federation of State High School Associations
Room 1240
7 South Dearborn Street
Chicago, Illinois 60603

COLLEGE

College Athletics Publishing Service
349 East Thomas Road
Phoenix, Arizona 85000

AMATEUR

Amateur Athletic Union of the United States
3400 West 86th Street
Indianapolis, Indiana 46268

PROFESSIONAL

The Sporting News
P.O. Box 56
St. Louis, Missouri 63166

glossary

Air dribble: Throwing or tapping the ball into the air and then touching it before it hits the floor.

All-court press: A press applied by the defensive team all over the court, not only in the offensive team's frontcourt as in the half-court press. Another term for this is all-floor press.

Arc: The trajectory of the ball in flight.

Assist: Any maneuver that helps a teammate to a score.

Backboard: The board supporting the baskets at either end of the court.

Backcourt: That half of the court which includes the basket a team is defending. Once a team acquires possession of the ball, it is allowed ten seconds to get the ball from the backcourt to its frontcourt.

Backcourtman: One of the team's better ballhandlers who develops a team's offense.

Back-in: When a pivotman is backstepping toward the basket, with or without the ball, and he makes contact with a defender; a foul should be called on the pivotman.

Back-tap: When a player taking a jump ball taps the ball back toward the basket that he is defending.

Back-up drill: A defensive player forces one of his teammates in possession of the ball to move in the direction he wants him to go. This practice drill will help the defensive player develop his techniques.

Bank shot: The ball caroms, or angles off the backboard into the basket.

Baseball pass: The ball is thrown with an overhand motion similar to a baseball catcher's throw to second base.

Blocking out: Keeping your opponent away from the basket in a rebounding situation.

Batting the ball: An attempt on the part of an offensive or defensive player to gain possession of the ball by batting it in the direction of a teammate. Batting the ball with a closed fist is a violation.

Behind-the-back dribble: The dribbler passes the ball around him with either his right or left hand and picks it up with the other hand.

Bigman: The pivotman, or center, usually the tallest player on the team if he's a good shooter.

Captain: The player elected by his teammates or designated by the coach to lead the team.

Center: A forward who plays the center area of the court. He is also referred to as the bigman or pivotman.

Center restraining circles: The circles at the center of the court, one within the other.

Change of pace: An offensive player changes from a slow speed to a fast speed in an attempt to shake himself free from his defensive man.

Or, when a defensive player bursts into sudden speed in an attempt to steal the ball from an offensive player.

Charge: An offensive player runs into or brushes up against a defensive player. This is considered a personal foul.

Chaser: In a zone defense, the front player who runs after the ball and follows it, pressuring the offensive player who has possession.

Cheap basket: A goal obtained through poor defense rather than good offensive plays. Sometimes called garbage goals.

Check: To stop an opponent temporarily without physical contact.

Clear out: A maneuver in which the offensive players move out of an area taking their defensemen with them, so that the man with the ball will have a chance for an open shot.

Clear-the-boards: To grab a rebound.

Clog: When the entire offensive team is under the basket making it difficult for the pivotman to shoot.

Clutch shooter: A player who can score when the pressure is on.

Contact: Touching an opponent.

Control the boards: Being able to get most of the rebounds, thus creating a better chance to win the game.

Cornerman: A player who stays near the corners to be able to receive a pass for a shot from the man in the middle.

Corner shot: Any shot taken from the corner of the court near where the sideline meets the end line.

Crashing the board: Heading toward the backboard every time a shot is taken to pick up the rebound.

Cross-court pass: Any pass thrown laterally, from one sideline to the other. This pass is easy to intercept.

Crossover: A step used by an offensive player in changing direction, particularly in dribbling, where one foot crosses the other.

Defensive board: The backboard that a team is defending.

Defensive triangle: A formation where three defensive men form a triangle between their basket and their opponents. The purpose of this triangular formation is to capture the rebound by legally preventing the offense from moving in toward the basket after a shot.

Deliberate foul: A play in which the defensive man intentionally causes his opponent to foul him.

Discontinue: To dribble, stop, and then dribble again. This is a violation, penalized with loss of ball.

Double dribble: Dribbling a second time after the first dribble has ended. This is a violation, penalized with loss of ball.

Double pivot: Two offensive men positioned near the basket.

Double screens: Two offensive players move between a teammate and his opponent, or behind a teammate's opponent to block the defensive man.

Double-teaming: Two defensive players gang up on the offensive man who has the ball. The objective is to prevent a shot, pass, or dribble. Many times the defense gets the ball through this maneuver.

Dribble: Bouncing the ball on the floor while moving. The offensive player who has the ball must bounce it as he moves or he will be penalized with loss of ball. If a forward is dribbling for a shot, he is allowed a step and a half before he releases the ball.

Drive: When an offensive player is dribbling the ball toward the basket.

Dunk: Dropping the ball into the basket from directly above. You need good jumping ability to get above the rim and large hands to control the ball.

End line: Runs the width of the rectangular court and joins the sidelines to form the court boundary.

Face guard: An illegal maneuver, occurring when a defensive man guards a pivotman from the rear. In order to prevent the pivotman from receiving the ball, the defensive man places his hand in front of the pivotman's eyes to obstruct his vision. This is legal if it accidentally happens when *your* man has possession of the ball.

Fake: A feint to throw your opponent off guard. Can be a fake shot, fake before a pass, or fake dribble; also a head fake, body fake, or foot fake.

Fast break: The defensive team suddenly gains possession of the basketball through an interception or rebound and immediately starts toward its offensive basket in an attempt to score.

Feeder: The offensive player who passes the ball into the bigman or player who has been scoring consistently.

Field goal: A score counting two points, made when the ball is shot through the basket.

Fingertip control: The ability to control the ball in a shot, pass, or dribble by using the tips of the fingers and not the palms.

Flick: A quick, light flip of the wrist in passing or shooting the ball.

Flip pass: A short overhand pass that is executed with a flick of the wrist, and often used by the pivotman.

Floor position: The position of the players on the court.

Follow through: The continuation of a player's forward momentum after he has released the ball. Follow through is also important in passing to help get the ball directly to the receiver.

Follow up: When a player heads for the basket and the rebound as soon as he takes his shot.

Forced shot: A hurried shot taken by a player who is being closely guarded and does not take his normal time to shoot.

Forwards: The offensive players.

Foul: An infraction of the rules; the referees are responsible for calling all fouls.

Foul trouble: A player must leave the game when he has committed five fouls.

Free-style play: A term applied to a team that has no set offensive system, but permits the various members of the team to maneuver the ball at their own discretion. Also called free-lance play.

Free throw: One or more free throws may be awarded a player or a team after a personal foul, technical foul, or combination of the two. The free throw shooter is permitted ten seconds to shoot from the fifteen-foot line without any defensive interference.

Free-throw lane: The area under the basket extending from the endline to the circular area some nineteen to twenty feet away.

Free-throw line: The line dividing the free throw circle in half and parallel to the endline. A player takes his free throw shot from behind the line. He must stay there until the ball hits the rim of the basket.

Freeze: A term applied when the leading team attempts to maintain possession of the ball while letting the clock run out.

Fronting: A defensive term used when the defending player does not permit any man, teammate or opponent, to come between him and the man he is guarding.

Frontcourt: That half of the court which includes the basket a team is shooting toward for goals.

Fumble: To lose control of the basketball momentarily.

Give-and-go: When one member of the offensive team passes the ball to a teammate and cuts for the basket to receive a return pass. The player who starts the play passes (gives) and immediately heads for the basket (goes).

Goal: When a player scores by shooting the ball through the basket.

Guards: The defensive members of a team.

Gunner: A player who shoots more often than he should and who rarely passes to a teammate.

Hacking: A foul by a defensive player when he slaps or hits an offensive player with his hand in an attempt to prevent a shot.

Half-court press: The defensive players pressure the ball in their opponent's frontcourt.

Handoff: Passing the ball quickly to a teammate moving with or toward you. This is a short pass, not more than 3 feet.

Hands-up defense: A defensive player keeps at least one, if not both, hands raised so the offensive player will not be able to get a good sight on the basket.

Held ball: When two or more opponents have their hands so firmly on the ball that neither can gain possession without undue roughness.

High dribble: A dribble in which the ball is bounced at waist level or higher.

Hook pass: A ball-handling maneuver where the ball is thrown to a receiver with a hooking, or flipping, motion of the arm, similar to the hook shot.

Hook shot: A player shoots over his head with the arm that is farther from the basket.

Hoop: The basket.

Inbounds: A term applied to the area within the court.

Interception: When a defensive player steals the ball from the opposition by grabbing a pass intended for an opponent.

Isometric: A term applied to exercises performed against resistance, resulting in marked increase of muscle tone without significant shortening of muscle fibers.

Jackknife: A jumping position performed by a rebounder in mid-air The arms and legs are forward, while the body is bent with the rear end extended.

Jam-up: When a defensive team clogs the middle of the court.

Jump ball: A procedure for putting the ball in play at the beginning of the game or during the game, in which the referee throws the ball up between two opponents, one of whom succeeds in tapping it to a teammate.

Jump shot: The shooter jumps up in the air, coming off both feet, and shooting at the height of his jump.

Keyhole, or key: The entire free throw area, including the foul line, the top of the foul circle, and the free-throw lane.

Lateral pass: A pass to the side rather than forward or backward.

Lay-up: A shot taken right next to the basket, using the backboard as a banking surface.

Lead pass: A pass that is thrown ahead of the intended receiver, so that he will be able to catch it as he maintains a running speed.

Lob pass: A slow arcing pass. Sometimes used to feed a pivotman when he is standing behind his defenseman.

Low dribble: A ball bounced close to the floor.

Lunge: In a attempt to get possession, a defenseman moves forward toward the ball, throwing himself off-balance and leaving himself in an awkward position for a split-second offensive attack.

Man-for-man: A style of defense where each member of the defensive team plays a certain man on the offensive team and tries to keep him from scoring.

Middleman: The offensive player in the center of a fast break.

Midline: The center line that separates the frontcourt from the back-court.

Offensive board: The backboard or goal that a team is attacking.

One-hand shot: A shot taken with one hand.

Out-of-bounds: A term applied to the out-of-court area. Play stops when the ball goes out-of-bounds.

Out-of-bounds play: A player passes the ball to a teammate from out-of-bounds, and the rest of the team handles the ball according to a prearranged plan.

Overshift: In a zone defense, when the defensive players move too far to the left or right leaving part of the area under the basket open for a shot.

Over-the-shoulder pass: A pass that is thrown backward over the shoulder.

Palming the ball: A violation occurring when a player turns his wrist and hand as he dribbles, enabling him to protect and control the ball between bounces.

Percentage shot: A particular shot that an offensive player is most successful at completing.

Peripheral vision: The ability of a player to observe what is happening on both sides of him without turning his head.

Personal foul: A foul that results from body contact between two or more players on opposing teams.

Pick: Creating an open shot by screening off another player. This also is called a block.

Pitch out: A pass from a rebounder underneath the basket to a team-mate away from the basket. This is usually the first pass on a fast break.

Pivoting: When the player with the ball is standing still, but wishes to move in a circular fashion either before or after he dribbles, he keeps one foot stationary and turns on it, while moving the other foot.

Pivotman: An offensive player positioned near the basket to receive a pass and make a shot. He also is called the center or bigman.

Playmaker: An offensive player who sets up plays.

Possession: Control of the ball.

Press: A maneuver performed by the defensive team to make it diffi-cult for the opposition to move the ball while attempting to score.

Rebound: A missed shot that hits the backboard.

Rebounder: A player who takes possession of the ball as it's rebounding.

Referees: The two officials in charge of the game. One is the chief referee and has complete control of the game in case there is a disagreement.

Reserve: Substitute player.

Reverse dribble: Changing direction while dribbling.

Saline solution: A salt and water solution taken after practicing or playing to replace salt lost in the body through perspiration.

Scoring: Making points.

Screen: A maneuver used by the offensive team to set up a player for scoring by blocking the defensive man without making contact.

Set offense: The play that the offense uses after the fast break has failed or if the fast break opportunity does not arise.

Shooting area: That part of the floor from which most of a team's shots are made.

Shovel pass: An underhand pass thrown with two hands.

Sideline: The two parallel lines running the length of the court and meeting the end lines to form the boundary.

Stalling: Maintaining possssion of the ball without taking a shot while the clock is running out or while waiting for a good shooting opportunity.

Steps: See *traveling*.

Stuff shot: See *dunk*.

Tap-in: A shot off a rebound, occurring when a player taps the ball toward the rim.

Technical foul: A foul called on a player by the referee because of some form of unsportsmanlike conduct. This does not count toward the total fouls that a player is allowed before being disqualified.

Ten-second rule: The offensive team has to move the ball from its backcourt to its frontcourt within ten seconds after gaining possession of the ball.

Three-on-two: A play situation when the offensive team outnumbers the defensive team by three to two.

Three-point play: When a player making a field goal is fouled while shooting, yet makes the shot for two points, and then converts the free throw into a third point.

Three-second lane: The foul lane under the basket where an offensive player can remain for three seconds before shooting.

Throw-in: When the ball is put into play by throwing it to a teammate from out-of-bounds.

Time-out: A one-minute period during which play is stopped and teams are permitted strategy discussions.

Trailer: A forward who follows behind the play.

Traveling: A violation of the rules in which more than one and a half steps are taken before the ball is dribbled. This also is called walking, running, and steps.

Turkey: A poor player.

Turn shot: A shot taken as a player turns toward the basket.

Under-the-arm pass: A short, one-hand pass flipped under the arm.

Violation: Breach of the rules.

Voice commands: A way in which the defensive team can communicate when attempting to intercept the ball.

Walking: See *traveling*.

Work the ball: A term used to designate the offensive teamwork used to create a good opportunity for a shot.

Zone defense: A particular defensive formation in which the player covers an area of the floor rather than a particular player on the other team.

index